Exhausted

CHAOS

Finding yourself in pregnancy, love, and loss

Sarah Salopek

This book is dedicated to my ever-loving husband, and my wonderful sons.

Acknowledgments

Thank you to my husband for always showing up, no matter the situation. Without you, we wouldn't have our crazy little family and all the love within these walls. You've never let me give up on myself or us, as you are my person. I love you.

Contents

These Are My Footprints

These are my footprints,
so perfect and so small.
These tiny footprints
never touched the ground at all.

Not one tiny footprint,
for now I have my wings.
These tiny footprints were meant
for other things.

You will hear my tiny footprints,
in the patter of the rain.
Gentle drops like angels tears,
of joy and not from pain.

You will see my tiny footprints,
in each butterflies' lazy dance.
I'll let you know I'm with you,
if you give me just a chance.

You will see my tiny footprints,
in the rustle of the leaves.
I will whisper names into the wind
and call each one that grieves.

Most of all, these tiny footprints,
are found in mummy's heart,
cause even though I'm gone now,
we'll never truly part.

By Tamara Barker

Introduction

Independence is thought to be the unrealistic and socially accepted expectation that a person must be able to manage their own thoughts, burdens, and emotions all on their own. However, independence is defined, at least based on a web search from dictionary.com, as being free from another person or persons' control.

For as long as I can remember, I have been a very driven individual, with the false belief that I needed to push myself continuously and not ask for help or advice along the way. I had this notion that I had to do the hard pieces of life on my own, to prove that I was "independent." I was pushing myself to be someone who was "strong" based on society's terms. Ironic...because instead of being free from another person or persons' control, I was feeding into it and allowing society to dictate how I should live. I was very young and still had much to learn. As I've grown into who I am today as a woman, a mother, a wife…I've learned that this expectation is wrong to put on myself, as no one is meant to take on the burdens of the world single-handedly.

I'm proud to say that I was blessed with my mom's stubborn attitude and my dad's work ethic, which sound like the lyrics to an old country song. But with my parents inherited traits and the distorted reality of how independence should work, I thought I was ready to go into the world and was prepared for whatever came next. I've tried a hundred different ways in about as many different times to get these words onto paper, because I knew I needed too. I needed to write this down so that I could show women, parents, grandparents, siblings, aunts, uncles, family members, friends, and anyone who has ever felt the loss of a child that while it is absolutely not fair, it is survivable. But you cannot do it alone.

This is my story. This is how I survived and the lessons I've learned along the way. This book is not going to be easy to read. Not because of the big words and large philosophical mantras, but because these are my raw and honest moments on paper. This is my love letter to the NICU mama, my love letter to my boys, and my love letter to myself.

I have experienced things that no person should ever experience, but sadly, it happens more often than it should. I have loved, I have lost, I have experienced the raw moments of motherhood and the hardships of a marriage after losing a child. I have also seen my child thrive and grow to be the most amazing person, but I have also lost a piece of myself while learning to grow new parts of my soul. I am hoping this book can help you realize that while these things happen, it is not normal. It is not something a person can possibly prepare for, and don't ever let anyone tell you otherwise. But this is also about hope and learning to be your own best advocate...buckle up!

Chapter 1

Let's start at the beginning. I grew up in the smallish town of McKeesport, Pennsylvania, just as my father did. I've seen pictures and heard stories of what McKeesport was like when the steel mills were thriving in the early 1900s, but the steel industry began to collapse in the early 1980s. At this point as the collapse was occurring, my father had met my mother in Utah and brought her back to McKeesport to grow and raise their family. Although the industry collapse was causing the economy to fall, my mom was fortunate enough to experience the tail end of this era and would tell us about how Fifth Avenue used to have beautiful tall buildings that decorated each block, like uniquely placed gemstones to twinkle in the sunlight as a memory caught in time. She had told us of large department stores like Gimbles, G.C. Murphy's, and Jaison's. There was The Daily News on the main street, movie theaters, and endless restaurants to choose from during weekly outings. Sadly, McKeesport is now like the sad, forgotten old pair of shoes left in your closet. The shoes you hope would come back in style, but instead, all the other newer shoes are piled on top, and the old ones get discolored, squished, and ultimately forgotten.

I am blessed to be from a family of strong women, as I am the middle child of three daughters. My older sister's name is Heather, and my younger sister is Mandy. Growing up in McKeesport with parents like mine and three girls in the family, you learned quickly that family came first and how to be a fighter. I won't go into my parents' history, that is their biography and theirs alone to narrate for the world. However, their history did teach us to stand up for each other, how to work hard, and that no matter what mistakes you make, you are still loved. My sisters and I are all very different and unique individuals who went in, as I like to call it, a perfect equilateral triangle with the paths we've chosen in life. We are all exactly 60° from one another, never shifting closer and staying at that equidistant length on who we are. We will never be similar, but we love each other for our differences.

Heather has always been quiet but stouthearted, never wavering in her love for Japanese culture or protecting her family. On the opposite side of the triangle, Mandy has always been the outgoing and unreserved individual who will make a point to show who she is, especially if her way isn't the most accepted. My parents have taught us that no matter which way we veer, our sisters will be the ones to always have our back when we need them most. As parents usually are, they were right.

Then, there is Cheyan. Cheyan deserves her own story, as I could write volumes of our childhood and growing into adulthood together. The belly-aching comical stories I could tell, or the heartbreak and grief we've weathered together. We've been a part of each other's weddings, been there for our children being born, birthdays, holidays, funerals, break ups, and everything in between. When we were young, Cheyan used to live a couple of houses down from us when we all lived in McKeesport, and our parents were friends with one another. So, naturally, my sisters and I would play with Cheyan and her two younger brothers. Cheyan has been and always will be the 4th sister to our family. Through the years, she has shown me that the people who love you are there for you, especially when you are at your lowest. She is my person.

Now, for some additional background on how I came to be this stubborn individual. When I was a junior in high school, my dad accepted a new job out of state, but Heather remained in McKeesport with my grandmother so she could finish her senior year. For being a social butterfly, I had a hard time fitting in as I missed my old friends and being new to living on a farm as a 17 yr. old girl was lonely. As I hit my senior year of high school, Heather and I moved into an apartment together so that I could graduate from McKeesport High School. With the desire to graduate with my life-long friends, my parents didn't hesitate and helped to support my sister and me financially. This step gave me my first taste of self-sufficiency as I would go to classes during the day and then work at the local donut shop in the evenings and weekends. I thought that I would spend more time with my friends soaking up the last days of my childhood before high school graduation, but I had unintentionally thrust myself into balancing school and work and not as much play as I had hoped. I was always tired, worn out, and frustrated as my 18-year-old mind and body weren't prepared for this. Sadly, I would wear myself out and still refuse to ask for help or advice because of the belief I had that if I asked for help, I was failing at this practice run of adulthood. My family and friends may tell you that I can be a bit competitive and do not like to fail at anything. More on that later.

A few months before graduation, I ended up in an unhealthy relationship that, unfortunately, lasted throughout all 4 years of college. I don't need to go into the details here either, but we were wrong for each other in only ways you could imagine. Truthfully, it was my first serious relationship and not only was I young, but I was naive. I thought that the feelings I had developed was 'true love' and the awful ways we treated one another was how a relationship was supposed to be. Thankfully, we grow up and learn otherwise, and I was lucky enough to learn during our relationship that it wasn't love, but that it was a chemical change in our brains that make us feel like we're in love. When you start a new relationship, especially so young in life, your brain has actual physical changes it goes through when your attracted to someone else and hormones are released called dopamine, serotonin, and oxytocin. Once I learned the chemistry of attraction and that the terrible ways we had treated each other wasn't how you show love, I gained more self-confidence and took the steps I needed to leave him.

I read a book once by Rachel Hollis where she said there is a social norm that to be a good woman is to be good for other people, and that we need to be good for ourselves and not be afraid to stand up for our needs. Society and social media show us how easily people and their relationships are studied under these magnifying glasses when, realistically, it's no one's damn business. I was just starting to understand more of who I was at this point in my life; not just what I wanted but what I needed as a person and as a woman. When I started being honest with myself and understanding that the people who really love me would support my decision to leave him and focus on my future.

Once I graduated college, it was like I had found this new self-respect and assurance. I didn't need a relationship to feel whole. I didn't need a man to make me feel loved. I didn't need someone to tell me what career to choose or where I should live. I needed to be a good woman for myself. I discovered that I was my own person, and I was ready to own it. I decided that I wanted to start living my life and having fun while starting a career. So, I began dating and going out with old friends that I had lost touch with, ahem, Cheyan. I had started working as a temporary contractor within a chemical company and slowly built the foundation of my career.

I had grown into a very self-reliant woman who worked her way through college, having two jobs and full semesters. Just like my senior year of high school, I didn't have much of a college life, to be honest. In my 4 years of education, I went to maybe a handful of parties or nights at the bar but was usually working, asleep, or watching NCIS as I was exhausted from my busy schedule. This self-reliance gave me my perspective for that phase in my life and who I would eventually become.

Chapter 2

I'm hoping my kids read this someday and know how loved they have always been. I want them to know how amazing their dad is and how knowing the right ways to love someone can influence your entire life for the better.

Before I met my husband, their father, I did not want kids. Absolutely not. Now, let me state this: my parents are amazing and truly gave us a fantastic childhood with lots of love. I do not have many unhappy childhood memories, as they are filled with late-night sleepovers, swimming parties, bike rides in the playground behind our house, and all the silly ways we would get in trouble that we still laugh about. However, growing up you also think about the next steps in life and what you do or do not want. When it came to kids, I thought about losing my newfound freedom to a child who would demand my time, I didn't want to give that up. The thought of bringing something so precious into a world that has so much heartbreak, I just couldn't imagine it. I knew I had a lot of love to give, and I loved my two beautiful nieces so absolutely, but I wasn't ready to open myself in this way. Truthfully, after some late-in-life self-reflection, I strongly believe it was because of the unhealthy relationship I had been in during the years prior. I couldn't bring a child into a world where all I had known was this unhealthy type of connection to another person. Absolutely not.

Truth be told, when I started dating my husband, Shawn, it was really the first time I thought of starting a family. We had an instant connection the night we met. I believe it's because we both have strong personalities, and we've always fully accepted one another and who we are as people. The first time I thought about maybe wanting kids was because there was something about him and the way he was so genuine. Shawn has never sought acceptance for who he is and has always unapologetically been himself. While also very frustrating, this has always been my favorite trait of his, and I wanted more of him. A couple little Shawn's running around…how fulfilling it would be to give more of my love to him.

When Shawn and I got married in October 2014, we decided we were going to wait to have children. I knew how badly he wanted to be a dad; it was like his purpose in life was to be a father. But I was still afraid of losing my freedom and being on demand to this little human. I liked my time alone with my new husband. I liked having my own schedule. I liked being able to sleep in and go out when I wanted. So, we decided on a compromise. We would wait to get pregnant until our first wedding anniversary. This was so that we had that first year of marriage together to just be "us." Since our anniversary was in October, I was fully expecting to have the start of a cute little swollen belly by November of the following year, or at least the secret between us that we could share 12 weeks later. However, we learned the hard way that you cannot plan anything in life. Don't even try.

It wasn't a full year of marriage when we had gone on a family vacation with my in-laws. We went to Ocean City, Maryland, and we were both anxious about starting a family. Even though we still had a few months before we hit our first anniversary, the possibilities were making us giddy with excitement. One night, while lying in our room in the condo, we were whispering about having a baby so that the others couldn't hear. We decided to be spontaneous and decided to start trying to have a baby when we got home from vacation. Now, if you know us, Shawn and I are not actually spontaneous people. We typically talk about a subject for quite a long time to convince both of ourselves that it's the right choice before we end up pulling the trigger and diving in. For example, we talked about having a baby for 10 months, not realizing that August was only 2 months before our anniversary, and we weren't being very spontaneous at all. We had thought this out long and hard, and we were ready. We were both so excited and ready to start this adventure into parenthood...the swollen belly, the cravings, the nursery, the books, the little feet, and buying clothes for this tiny person. So, the journey began.

The following week after vacation, we decided we would wing it, and it would happen when it happened. That's when I felt my life turn into a funnel. Not the type of clear glass funnel you use in a laboratory where you can see what is happening inside, but the dark plastic funnel you use to add oil to your car to keep it running. You feel so open and clear-headed at the top when you start, ready to take on as much as possible. But, as time goes on, the opening gets narrower, and less and less fits through. Your purpose gets clouded, and eventually, that funnel gets clogged because of too much compression within the neck.

I could feel when funnel began to tighten…month after month of anxiously hoping I wouldn't get my menstrual cycle; I began to feel disheartened. I would anticipate my cycle, praying it wouldn't happen and pushing myself to believe that the cramps I felt coming on were signs of implantation, but it always came. After several months, I began to go crazy. I call this type of craziness "The Fertility Hysteria." By my definition, fertility hysteria is when a woman is ready to bear children and begins to slowly lose her mind in the process of attempting to become pregnant. The type of mania that many women trying to or have tried to have a child would understand…. It is the compulsion of downloading the endless period tracking and ovulation applications, thinking that the more you have on your cell phone, the more likely you are to actually get pregnant. Please note that these two things in no way correlate to one another. Every single day, I was googling ovulation or early pregnancy symptoms, buying ovulation tests, and the gel that was supposed to help the sperm live longer and get to the egg faster. Sex became more of a scheduled assignment than an enjoyable experience with your partner. It quickly became all I ever talked about with my husband, and it was running our lives. We would obsess over what it would be like to have a little one saying "mama" and "dada;" how cute it would be for our dog to snuggle him or her, and what our parenting styles would be for a child that didn't seem to be coming our way. I even remember that when we would see someone else share their happy news of having a child, the unfair resentment we would both have towards them would show its ugly head. And man, it really was ugly. As if, they were doing it out of spite. It didn't logically make sense, but there it was. This is not the type of people we were, holding resentment for someone else's joy. So, we both began to fall into this gray cloud, the sadness and tears every 4 weeks like clockwork. Intimacy continued to become more of a chore than affection for one another.

After almost 10 months of consistently trying and feeling like my body was failing, Cheyan talked us into going to the same fertility clinic that had helped her and her husband conceive their first daughter. It took some persuading for Shawn, but he finally agreed to go and at least check it out. I called the next morning to make an appointment.

When we walked into the office, it was very intimidating. There were two other couples sitting in the waiting room, no one talking, everyone's eyes on their phones or the floor and no one wanted to look at each other. There was this large TV hanging towards the left side of the office near the door that would take you back to the rooms. The TV was on a loop shuffling through pictures of babies that they had successfully helped couples conceive. The area we were sitting in out front looked as though the décor was an attempt at something supposed to bring comfort with the soothing green colors with tan accents. But it was like we all knew what the other was thinking or feeling, and that we were all secretly ashamed or embarrassed for being there. Why was there this terrible stigma that we were broken or there was something wrong with us because we needed help? I was angry that anyone would feel this way. Let me tell you, ladies, this is bullshit. This isn't the 1950s, the stigma is in our own heads even though it's been gone for generations. These things are openly discussed, supported, and infertility is way more common than you realize nowadays. You may think that society believes there is something wrong with us, but that is simply not true. It is created from our own personal doubts and fears that we are not good enough and must be able to do everything on our own. Ladies. We cannot and should not put this type of pressure on ourselves, as we are human. If a couple is having an issue getting pregnant and openly talk about it, there is far less judgement and more empathy than you realize. And if people judge you and your womb, they do not need to be a part of you, or your womb's lives.

The next piece of shame I was carrying with me over those months leading up to this appointment was the guilt

I felt that the reason we may not have a child was my fault. What if it was my body that wasn't working properly? The concern washed over me like an uncomfortable swell for the guilt I undoubtedly also knew Shawn would have if it was something with his fertility. It was truly too much emotion for one morning. Even with my second cup of coffee and my husband by my side, I was ready for these doctors to wave their magical speculums and tell us that my healthy uterus and Shawn's valiant sperm were only missing each other by minutes.

I tried to give a tight smile at another woman who made eye contact with me for a moment, but she quickly dropped her eyes to the floor.... Trying to get out of my own head, I looked over; Shawn was playing a game on his phone very calmly and ignoring the other couples. When each person would talk to their partner, they kept their heads down and whispered. It was so unnecessarily awkward. This is normal. Infertility, unfortunately, is not that uncommon. Infertility is not something to be ashamed of, and we need to lift each other up and support one another. We shouldn't be looking at the floor. We shouldn't have our heads down. We need to lift our heads up high and be ready to accept kindness and respect from one another; no one needs to go this alone. This is not independence, and we need support from other people.

After a while, a woman called us back and put us into a tiny 10'x10' room with a round table, three chairs, some pictures of women's reproductive systems, an anatomically accurate hard plastic uterus on the table, and a framed BMI chart leaning against the wall. We waited and waited. We waited for hours to see the doctor, and then we waited some more. Shawn was highly irritated as waiting for a physician is not one of his stronger traits, but I kept trying to make jokes and lighten the mood. The realization, that infertility was more common than I had imagined had set in; we weren't the only ones there. We were just one of many couples that needed help to conceive a baby. At this point, I knew this was bigger than magical OB/GYN instruments and there could truly be a problem with one of our reproductive systems.

The real down and dirty truth is, while the human body is amazing…it is also not perfect and can absolutely let you down when you need it to function properly. This isn't your fault either; this is anatomy, its science. This is life. I mean, look at where I was at that moment. After everything we've tried, I had that guilt of not being able to get pregnant because my anatomy wasn't ready or not functioning the way I thought it should be. The guilt I felt was not logical, but I didn't know that in the moment. The feelings I had were completely valid. But the guilt over something you cannot control, is just not logical. The thoughts that I had were not just the guilt of letting Shawn down, but maybe I wasn't meant to be a mom. My mind then went darker and then began telling me that maybe I wasn't meant to be the wife of this great guy that is meant to be a dad; maybe I'm the failure here. And I don't like to fail.

Chapter 3

If you have ever been through infertility or went to a fertility clinic, there is a whole range of emotions that you experience that weren't on the welcome brochure. First, is the feeling of being disconnected from reality. It is like you are on the outside of your body, watching yourself as a stranger, trying to comprehend what is happening before you can accept that this is your new reality. After the doctor reviews the reproductive charts, the plastic replica of a woman's genitals, and reads through the stack of paperwork, you feel like you're signing away your medical rights to a car dealership. Then, you slowly come back to reinhabit your body and start to perceive the actuality of what you need to do.

On our long list of to-dos was to complete various amounts of paperwork, have blood work done for a wide range of hormones, test sperm count and motility, receive internal and external ultrasounds, and then have this uniquely painful process done where the doctor pushed saline and air into my cervix so that they could see how the air bubbles float through my fallopian tubes to make sure they were open. I think I provided everything possible, including my dog's eye color and my sister's first car make and model. The diagnosis…nothing physically wrong that could be determined; however, they were clinically diagnosing me with PCOS or polycystic ovarian syndrome. PCOS is actually quite common from what I've read and heard from friends, but I also feel that PCOS is sometimes used as a default diagnosis for infertility when nothing else can be confirmed. Don't get me wrong, PCOS is absolutely a real disorder, however, I feel that sometimes it's too easily given to women because there's a reason why they haven't been able to get pregnant, but the lab results came back within normal ranges. My hormones came back okay, my menstrual cycle was consistent, but I was still having difficulty getting pregnant. I was willing to accept this diagnosis since there were treatments available that could help my fertility.

Once all the testing was complete, we went in for a follow-up appointment to discuss the next steps with our doctor, and what our treatment options were. The list reminded me of a menu with a la carte options, except without the a la mode. We began to review the first option, which was Clomid®. If you've never heard of Clomid®, it's a medication that needs to be carefully timed when you take it. On the second day of bleeding during your menstrual cycle, you start the round of pills that you take once a day for the next 5 days to encourage those little ovaries of yours to produce a mature egg so that it can be released about 10-12 days after your last pill into your uterus to be fertilized. The process really wasn't bad, but it was just more of the mundane tracking and out-of-body feelings that this couldn't really be my life.

After taking Clomid® for 5 days, your doctor encourages you to have sex every other day. Very romantic. But the guidance behind this is that sperm are slow swimmers and can live inside your body for a couple of days while they search around for that egg like a canary in a coal mine. However, they do warn you not to have sex daily because you need your partner's sperm count to have the chance to increase over 48 hours so that more swimmers are inserted at one time. Truthfully, that first month of scheduling sex with my husband was so uncomfortable. It felt more like a chore than being intimate, and how can you be in the mood when all you can think of is sperm count? Then, the dreaded wait that month to see if I was pregnant…I was not. We repeated this cycle again the following month, and I was still not pregnant. Then, our doctor told us that if it wasn't successful after the third round of Clomid®, we would need to take a break and then repeat the medication cycle in about six months. However, if we didn't want to wait another six months, there were other options we could explore. These were way more expensive and something we honestly just couldn't afford. But the other options were intrauterine insemination (IUI), where the doctors manually insert your husband's sperm into your uterus, or in-vitro fertilization (IVF), where the doctor removes the egg from your body, fertilizes it and puts it back. Neither of these options have guaranteed results, but knowing our goals, we would have chosen those options if we could have, but we are hard-working middle-class people and we knew this wasn't a logical option for us. No matter how badly we wanted to have a child.

Everything was so rigid, but I was grateful for someone else to help us keep track of this insanity. As we were entering into our third month of Clomid® and feeling utterly defeated, we decided to buy a puppy. Yes, a puppy. We were convinced that we weren't meant to be parents now and should just get an 8-week-old English bulldog puppy to love on. We already had a dog at home, Delta, but thought that this little creature would fill our void and give Delta a companion. Honestly, in hindsight, it was one of the best decisions we ever made, she was a great dog. When we brought her home, we named her Dixie and they became best friends right away. Having them to focus on allowed for some of the stress to be alleviated as we enjoyed our new twosome during that third month we were taking Clomid®.

Do you remember that welcome brochure at the fertility clinic, the one with the different emotions that weren't included in it? Well, the second emotion in my journey was doubt. After I completed that third round of Clomid® and woke up on the day I was supposed to start my menstrual cycle, I took a pregnancy test instead of giving myself a chance to miss my period. It, my friends, was positive. December 3rd, 2016, was the first day I found out I was pregnant. Now, let me back up a bit.... Shawn was working night-turn, so we had to fit in our regularly scheduled programming in between when I came home from work and him leaving for work a few hours later. I had woken up earlier than usual on a Saturday before Shawn got home, so I took the test. I remember that feeling of my stomach leaping into my throat and my heart physically skipping a few beats when I saw two blue lines immediately appear. I was nervous, I was shaking. I was doubtful. Now, with this being my first ever positive test, I was very fidgety and out-of-sorts in trying to figure out my next steps, almost manic. I felt like I couldn't sit still and I needed to constantly be moving. After I caught my breath, I called the fertility clinic office, as you're supposed to after you receive a positive test. They told me to come in that morning for a blood draw to check my hCG levels.

Not long after, Shawn walked through the front door from a long night at work and I was standing in the living room, practically bouncing as he walked in. I was standing next to our buffet holding a card I had bought on Etsy almost 18 months before in anticipation of a pregnancy announcement that I expected to happen right after we decided to get pregnant. It read "Husband, I have referred to you as many different things since we met.... I've been seeing this guy, this is my boyfriend, meet my fiancé.... Well, you're getting a new name, and you better get used to it, because you're going to be hearing it a lot!" Then, when you open the card, it says "Daddy" with a picture of a smiling sperm. I thought it was hilarious, but Shawn's face was a mix of exhaustion from working all night, and then pure confusion. This whole process had ruined this announcement for me and for the reaction I was expecting. I ended up being very bitter that morning as I drove to the clinic, logically knowing why Shawns reaction was less than imagined. It was supposed to be a scene from a rom-com where we fall in love and decide to have a baby, have crazy excited sex, take a test a few weeks later, and then tell him it was positive while we cried and danced around the kitchen. Nope, life is not a movie storyline.

We had to take this long journey to get here, and our announcement turned into a quiet doubtful morning while we drove to the fertility clinic. Shawn waited in the car so he could close his eyes, and I told him I would only be in the office for a few minutes. When we got home, I stalked my online chart for the results, and when I saw that my hCG levels were highly elevated, I had to wake Shawn up to tell him the good news! I, then, had to wait the longest week of my life to go back to get more blood work to make sure my hCG levels were increasing, which they were! Now cue the third emotion, euphoria.

We did it! We actually did it…. I was undoubtedly pregnant. After the thousands of ovulation tests, the tens of negative pregnancy tests, the poking, the prodding, the crying…I was pregnant. After 8 weeks, we went back into the fertility clinic for our routine tests to make sure I was maintaining the pregnancy. Sadly, this was the first time I had seen Shawn truly hopeful, now that it was something he could physically see on a screen in front of him, something almost tangible. The ultrasound tech was on my right side down by my hip, and Shawn was sitting on my left side holding my hand with both of his. When I looked over at him, his big brown eyes were watery as he looked at that screen of his little bubble worm floating around in my belly. That's when Shawn suddenly stood up, leaning over me so he was closer to the screen, pointing and yelled, "Is that two babies?! Right there?!" I thought he was losing his mind, and so did the ultrasound tech. Ironically, when Shawn would talk about his dream of being a dad and having kids, he had always wanted identical twin boys, so I thought he was imagining it or was trying to tease me. Well, we weren't at that point in this journey yet, but the ultrasound technician leaned into the screen and made a sound as she sucked in air and said, "Oh My God, it is!" I faintly remember yelling, "What?! Wait, no, no, it isn't!" over Shawn laughing hysterically with tears streaming down his face. He didn't have just a simple tear roll down his cheek, but full-on happy crying. That euphoric feeling that I had was now conflicted with fear…two babies?! The fertility doctor we had been meeting with came out to talk with us and let us know that now that they can confirm that I am pregnant with twins, due on August 10th, which is also my dad's birthday. All finally felt right in the world and cosmic fate had brought us to this point. The doctor then advised that I would need to follow up with my OB/GYN and a maternal-fetal medicine doctor, also known as MFM.

On the way home we decided to get lunch and kept talking about all the cute ways we would get to see our kids grow up together and be best friends. With how excited my husband was, I told him to pick anywhere for lunch since we needed to celebrate. Shawn's favorite celebratory meal...pizza. We stopped at the local pizza place for Shawn to get his favorite pepperoni rolls, while I made sure to eat a salad since I would be growing two humans now. The following Monday, I called my OB/GYN to make my follow-up appointment for the end of my first 12 weeks. This, my friends, is where our struggle and joy did another flip upside down.

Chapter 4

When Shawn and I walked into our 12-week appointment at my normal OB, we were giddy with excitement. We felt lighter, everything made us laugh, and we felt so in love. I had started to feel as though I was getting rounder, which I wasn't sure if that was common or not, since I was carrying multiples. Once the doctor came in and congratulated me, he then started talking through the MFM process again. He explained that they were referring me to that type of specialty doctor because multiples in a pregnancy could cause complications and they wanted their input for the best treatment plan. Great, I was in. When we left there, we made the appointment with the MFM, which got us in later that week. Let me tell you, my MFM doctor was the absolute kindest, caring, and most intelligent woman that I had ever met. When this small statured woman walked into the room, she brought a sense of calm with her. I laid on the table and lifted my shirt while the ultrasound technician tucked a white napkin into the top of my waistband and squirted the warm gel on my lower belly. And there they were, our sweet little bubble worms, which now looked like they were turning into gummy bears with arms and legs. It was an amazing feeling watching my children float around this warm and cushy bed my body made for them, and it was up to me to keep them safe.

Once the ultrasound was done, my doctor proceeded to tell us that I was pregnant with Mono/Di twins. This means that the babies were in the same placenta but separate amniotic sacs. This was good and bad news. The good news was: mono/mono twins are exceptionally dangerous, and thankfully, we didn't need to worry about one of their umbilical cords strangling the other. The bad news was: they still shared one placenta instead of it splitting into two separate ones, so they shared a circulatory system. She continued to tell us that I was now considered a high-risk pregnancy and would be followed closely because this was a rarer pregnancy type of multiples and the blood supply in mono/di twins is usually irregular. I remember asking if the Clomid® caused this since it increases ovulation, but she firmly reassured me that I would then have two mono/mono babies in separate placentas. The type of twins we had happens by chance when the cells are dividing around day 5 of fertilization. I felt slightly relieved that this wasn't our "fault," in taking medication to create babies we put at risk. However, she proceeded to tell us that due to the shared circulatory system, the fluid in the baby's amniotic sacs wasn't as evenly distributed as it should have been. At this point, she also told us she wasn't concerned and that it could even out later, but I was to come back in two weeks for another check.

Shawn and I left that appointment a little defeated and uneasy, but we also didn't let it phase us much because it didn't seem like something terrible could happen. We knew we would take anything that came our way head-on, and that was what we did. So, we waited the two weeks and went back when I was just over 14 weeks and repeated the same steps…shirt up, napkin in waistband, warm gel, and in came my MFM doctor. She still wasn't happy with the fluid, as they would measure the amount in centimeters and one baby had more than the other. My belly was showing more than you would think a 14-week pregnant woman would be, so I figured they were crazy that the fluid levels were low in one of the sacs. I kept thinking, "there has to be tons of fluid in there! Look at me, I'm huge!" I had even bought a few belly bands because I would lay on the couch in the evenings and cry because of how much pain I had in my hips and lower back. My body was changing so fast, at double the normal rate, and I felt it. My hips hurt to where I couldn't sit upright, my back felt like I fell down a flight of stairs, and my stomach constantly felt so bloated. Luckily, I didn't get any of the nausea or morning sickness symptoms; it was just the physical pain of expanding in time and space like a hot air balloon. The doctor reassured us that there was not a ton of fluid in there, and that it was more uneven than our last appointment. She sent us home and told us we would be able to know more in another two weeks, that we'd take it one step at a time.

At this point, we felt like it couldn't get any worse and it was going to correct itself. My body wouldn't fail me, again…fail me at getting pregnant, then fail me at keeping my babies safe. I had faith in my body; I had faith that I could control it by thinking positive thoughts and continuing like normal. But, once again, we cannot control these things, and it's not our fault for not being able to control them. This was a lesson you just eventually have to learn to accept, if you want to keep any of your sanity. However, I had not yet learned that my body's functions were not in my control. I couldn't use my non-existent telekinesis powers to channel my body into fixing the amniotic fluid between my children.

When we walked into that next appointment, all hell broke loose. I was 16 weeks pregnant to the day, and the amniotic fluid levels were more uneven than it was previously. Baby A had way too much fluid, and Baby B had barely enough. This is where the situation got even messier.

The doctor told us that we were officially being diagnosed with twin-to-twin transfusion syndrome (TTTS), and that we had approximately 1 week to have a specialized surgery called fetal laser photocoagulation (FLP) to try and save their lives. At the current fluid levels, one could pass from a stroke and the other could pass from cardiac arrest. The second caveat was that if one baby passed away, the other one would as well since their circulatory systems were connected. Our worlds came crashing down. Hard. We fought so hard for them to exist in our lives, that now we had to do everything we could to protect them and save their lives before they were even 5 months old in utero? How was this fair!? My husband and I are good people, and we were angry. So very angry. We were angry with the world, we were angry with God, we were even angry at ourselves. Why do bad things happen to good people? What we've learned since then…because they just do. It's not a cosmic force, it's not a divine punishment or test of your strength, and it's not because you did that one bad thing when you were a kid 10 years ago. The truth is that bad things just happen. The worst, unimaginable things happen for no ultimate reason. These things happen because it is a part of life, and learning to get through it is what helps you become a better fighter. Shawn and I knew the assignment was to protect our kids, so we put on our boxing gloves. Ding ding.

We only had one option of where we needed to go for this procedure as it's highly specialized, and that was Cincinnati Children's Hospital Medical Center. Our MFM doctor called them before we left that 16-week appointment to tell them we needed to be seen ASAP. Later that day, we were packing our bags to head to our appointment scheduled two days away. We were on a bit of a tight timeline with being given only a week, so we were heading out there the next day to prepare and wait, as we were terrified of what could happen between that moment and the appointment.

We both called our jobs to let them know we would be taking off the next couple of days and why, and thankfully, they were both very empathetic. But, as we were packing, my MFM doctor called me directly to tell me that there was a doctor who trained at the Cincinnati hospital for this procedure and now practices out of Magee-Women's Hospital. Hallelujah for living in Pittsburgh! Our access to all the different types of medical specialties is truly a blessing in this area. We called the phone number my MFM provided, and they were able to also get us in, in two days. We kept ourselves busy until that appointment. I was 16 weeks and 3 days when we walked in to meet the doctor. I'll refer to this remarkable man as Dr. Wright, which is not his actual name, but due to privacy, I do not want to impede his practice. However, it may do him some good to have some space in this book because he was truly extraordinary.

Before we met with the doctor, we were taken to a small dark room to have an ultrasound with the technician so that they could confirm the TTTS. Once it was confirmed, in walked Dr. Wright. He placed his large, sturdy hand on my belly and then looked at the screen and made the second confirmation. Coyly, he asked us if we would like to know the genders. You could tell this was his way of giving us a bit of happiness in a time of fear, so we both quickly said yes! Dr. Wright confirmed two identical twin boys. Shawn's dream had become a reality! We held each other's hands tightly as I got up and we walked to his office.

Dr. Wright welcomed us to make ourselves comfortable and had us sit in the chairs on the other side of his desk. Before he began, he brought a stethoscope to my chest and had me take the typical deep breaths. Then proceeded to take my blood pressure, which was surprisingly good for the situation we were currently in. He was silent for a moment, and I recall thinking how he was strikingly handsome and so large in stature for a man about to care for me and my tiny gummy bears. He spoke in a gentle but matter of fact way and began to tell us the honest reality of our situation, and the options were not good. We absolutely had twin-to-twin transfusion syndrome and needed to act quickly, as in the next 24 hours. Baby A had too much amniotic fluid and was at risk of cardiac arrest, while Baby B didn't have enough amniotic fluid and was at risk of a stroke. In both cases, it was not survivable because of the way their circulatory systems were connected and if one baby didn't survive, they would both pass away. The easiest and safest route, we were told, was to cut off the circulation to one of the umbilical cords and let that baby slowly die so that the blood pressure doesn't change too drastically and allow the other to thrive. The biological process would be that my body and the surviving baby would essentially absorb the one we had chosen to let go of. We understood what he was asking, but what the hell?! Literally, what the hell?! It was the meanest, most heartbreaking request we had ever heard, in the most soft-spoken tone with the best of intentions. How was this even an option? How was a parent, who had fought so hard for their children to exist, supposed to decide on which child lives and which child dies? Shawn and I looked at each other speechless, mortified, and knew that without either of us saying a word, this was not an option. Hell no!

Dr. Wright nodded and then got up and rechecked my heart and my blood pressure, which I found interesting. He explained that this process is not just dangerous for the babies but also for the mother. The amount of stress that twins put on a mother's body, compounded with the stress of making a decision of this magnitude, has been seen to turn critical for the mother. Thankfully, this wasn't the case as my heart rate was miraculously fine and my blood pressure normal. So, he continued to the next option, fetal laser photocoagulation (FLP).

What FLP basically is, is that the doctor takes a long tool and inserts it into your body and essentially into the placenta where they then use lasers to burn or seal off some of the veins in the circulatory system to make the distribution more even across both babies. By going in and lasering off some of the veins in the sac receiving too much fluid, it would give the second sac a chance to take on more nutrients. However, it was stressed to us over and over that this was a very rare and high-risk surgery. The biggest risk we were advised of is my water breaking prematurely or developing an infection. But what other options did we have? Either do nothing and lose both babies, intentionally let one of the babies die so the other could live or risk this surgery to save both of their lives. We knew the decision; we were going with FLP. Dr. Wright graciously understood and began the paperwork, as my surgery was the very next day. There was no time to lose, and we were to come in the very next morning and get prepped for surgery.

When we went home, we both were silent most of the night. Shawn held my hand tightly in his while he drove, and we didn't really speak. I think we were trying to digest the information we were given. And truly, I didn't think then about how hard this was on Shawn. I was so focused on my gummy bears and making it through the next 24 hours with both of them still alive. But, in hindsight, Shawn had to watch his wife take on this physical and mental burden and pray that his children survived. There was not much he could do but hold my hand as tightly as he was and love the three of us as fiercely as he did. I am truly so grateful that I had Shawn as my partner to get through this with, because I know that I couldn't have survived this if I didn't have such a strong person showing up for me.

The next day, when I was 16 weeks and 4 days pregnant, we parked in Magee's parking lot and began this next piece of the journey. We walked through the sliding glass doors and made our way over to the elevator bank. I believe it was the 3rd floor we were headed to, but at this point, I was completely on autopilot. I don't even remember the next couple of hours, as the next memory I have is the operating room. Another movie-like moment ruined...I did not go on a gurney and wave goodbye to my husband, as you see on screen where they are with you right up until the double swinging doors. Instead, Shawn stayed in the waiting room while I changed into a hospital gown and walked behind a nurse down a hallway and into this operating room, where I was asked to climb up and lie on the table. I was shaking so hard from a mixture of anxiety, fear, and being cold from the temperature in the room. As other people in the room walked around and prepped their stations, Dr. Wright came over and silently stood on my left side down towards my hip and watched everyone else in the room with me. He described to me that I would be numb but awake and then he pulled a blanket out of a warmer and laid it over me. I then felt that big burly hand rest on my stomach like an additional layer of amour. We were going to be okay.

There was a curtain placed at my chest, blocking my view down to my stomach, but I could see on the right side of my head, there were a couple of monitors, and a large computer screen that Dr. Wright would use to see the inside of the placenta for the procedure. I forgot to mention that I also had an anterior placenta, which means that it had attached to the front of my uterus, rather than the back side. What this means is that Dr. Wright needed to go around the placenta and up through the backside to be able to perform the procedure, which was an additional layer of difficulty during a very rare surgery. I think they had given me something for my anxiety, or maybe it was something with the local anesthetic, but I sure am glad that the next thing I remember is waking up in recovery. I slept through the whole procedure! I wasn't even really sore to be honest; it was like I had just taken a great nap. While I was sleeping peacefully, Shawn was waiting anxiously; thankfully, my mother-in-law brought him lunch and waited with him, but I was told the surgery was over pretty quickly. He came into the recovery room and Dr. Wright was there to tell us that the procedure went great, there were no complications, and I could go home the next day. They were able to laser some of the veins and even removed some of the amniotic fluid in Baby A's sac. He was leaving town that night, but I was staying the night in the hospital so that I could be monitored before going home. We were ecstatic and relieved.

Once we were taken up to our room for the night, we called both of our parents to let them know everything went okay. Shawn fell asleep quickly on one of the hospital chairs that pulled out into a bed, and I tossed and turned from side to back to side again. It was around 11:00 PM when I got up to go to the bathroom, that was when I wiped, and there was blood. My heart sank. I yelled for Shawn, and he called the nurse. Once the nurse came in, you could tell that she had never been exposed to a person with this type of operation before. After all, it was rare, and patients typically went to Cincinnati. I frantically asked, "What do I do?" and her calm response was, "I'll be back." But she didn't come back. I expected her to be back in the next 30 seconds, but we waited about 30-45 minutes before calling the nurse again and asked her to call Dr. Wright directly. Shortly after, my hospital room phone rang.

In his soothing voice, Dr. Wright asked me what was happening as he had already left town. I explained the situation to him, and he was empathetic but logical in reminding me that I did have a physical procedure done, and there could always be a little bit of blood. As long as it slowed down and stopped by morning, I could go home and relax. Done. I laid back down and tried my best to rest, but by the time morning came I was over tired and those hallmark puffy swollen eyes you get when it's too hot outside and you try to sleep without a fan on. But the bleeding had stopped so we went home. We sent our text messages and phone calls to let our families know we were home and doing well. Life then began to proceed back to normal…at least for a couple of days.

As I had mentioned before, my husband worked the night shift and later that week was a normal Friday night, and he was back to work. I had let the dogs out to go to the bathroom and made my way to bed…

Then, it happened. I was sound asleep on my back, the house was quiet and cool, and all of a sudden, I was jerked away in the pitch black of the night because I felt a weird pop inside my uterus and felt a large rush of liquid that did not come out of my bladder. I was frozen in fear. It happened; my water broke. It was around 1:00 am, and since we were technically into the next day, I was exactly 17 weeks pregnant. My first thought was "shit, I'm only 17 weeks pregnant, and my water broke." Immediately, I called my husband, who worked at a 911 center as a dispatcher about 30 minutes from home. When I told him my water broke, he was physically running out of the door on the other end of the phone to get home to me. Again, he always shows up.

I refused to move an inch let alone get out of bed; I was terrified and had so many unanswered questions in the moment. What actually happens when your water breaks? Am I about to go into labor? Are my babies about to slip out of my body since they're still so small at 17 weeks old? Are they even alive?

I continued to lay on my back perfectly still, not even moving my legs while I waited for Shawn. Within minutes, there was a knock at the door and Shawn called me on the phone to tell me an ambulance was outside. I was slightly annoyed and told him I couldn't get up to open the door because I didn't know what would happen, and that I didn't need an ambulance. Shawn made it home from work within 12 minutes. I know because it was the longest 12 minutes of my life. I stared at the clock on my cell phone, waiting, not moving, afraid to even breathe.

When Shawn got home, he didn't park in the driveway. He pulled his large silver Toyota Tacoma right up into the front yard, over the small concrete pad and parked directly in front of the door. He came rushing through that front door like he was going to war. However, no matter the situation, and I write this full of sincerity as I roll my eyes. I couldn't immediately get into the truck with leaking amniotic fluid. I had to wait until he laid a stack of towels on the seat and floor. I'm pretty sure he thought I was about to release a tidal wave in his truck.

At this point, I have never been so frozen in fear in my entire life. And I can say that as I write this book years after this all occurred, it was still one of the scariest moments of my life. I knew that full gestational pregnancies are delivered within 24 hours of a water breaking because there is a very high risk of infection. But my babies weren't full-term, and we were told that a fetus isn't viable until 23 weeks, but I was only 17 weeks. When

I say viable, what it means is that even with all the medical care in the world, a fetus cannot thrive outside of the mother's body when they are this young. I wanted to crawl up in that seat and let myself drown in that tidal wave my husband was expecting to ruin his interior.

My MFM doctor was about 30 minutes away at West Penn Hospital, so that is where we headed. The emergency room was full and when we told the triage nurse what was happening, they put us into a small side room for privacy. Some nurses and physician assistants came in and out to run a quick test using litmus paper to confirm it was in fact amniotic fluid and my water did break. At this point, it was a small but steady leak and once I sat on that table, I was not getting back up because I was afraid of what would happen if I did. We were exhausted and irritable because we had to wait for my MFM doctor until morning, as the ER did not give her a call as they were supposed to. She started at 9:00 am and once we got through the initial triage and tests, we ending up waiting 6 hours for her. We didn't know they didn't call her at the time, but I think our situation was so rare that people didn't know what to do with me.

When my MFM doctor walked in, she had tears in her eyes and her voice sounded strained as she tried to speak in a motherly tone. This was our fate. She explained that there was absolutely nothing they could do to fix a broken amniotic sac and our options were limited...we could either terminate then or go home and undoubtedly wait to go into labor within the next 24-48 hours.

Before going any further, I need to talk about this word 'options.' We were given options for fertility and TTTS treatments; we were given options for doctors and tests along the way. However, we were never given the option to choose the outcome, no matter what we thought was best. The word option is defined as a thing or things that may be chosen. But the truth is, you can give a person a hundred options, and each person needs to choose what is best for them and their situation. I cannot tell you the number of people who have asked me about my journey and then asked why we chose what we did or didn't choose. And well, it wasn't right for us. You can be given as many options as you want, but making a choice on what is best is still not easy. If two different women were put in the same situation, one might choose to go home and wait while the other chose to terminate. And that is okay! That is no one else's damn business. One of the best lessons I've learned in life is to stand by your decisions. So, if you were the mama with complications and had to make this tough choice and terminating was right for you, that is okay! Now, I'm not talking about taking sides on abortion rights or anything even close to that, but if your water had broken and you and your child were at risk of survival, I applaud you for using your best mama judgement and doing what was best for you and your child with the circumstances you had at that time.

I can't lie. At this point, I was so far beaten down and, for the slightest moment, I did consider the first option. And honestly, I didn't see this as giving up. We had been put into this boxing ring and taken every jab, hook, and uppercut we could take. My favorite movie series of all time is Rocky, and I felt like we had just lost a three-way match with Rocky Balboa and Clubber Lang. My MFM doctor walked out of the room so that we could talk and instead, we both silently cried. Neither of us made a sound; the tears just quietly poured down our faces. Shawn was sitting on one of those backless stools with wheels that was a couple feet lower than the table I was sitting on. He had put his left arm around my lower back, the right hand spread across my stomach as to hold his little family in his arms. His head was bent down laying on my right thigh as I felt my leg get wet with tears. My heart was shattered for this man that I love. His dreams of identical twin boys had happened and was slowly being taken away from him, from us. Our private conversation didn't last long; once we took a breath and could speak through the tears, we had made our decision. I was looking down at this man who was sitting on this backless uncomfortable stool for the last 6 hours tending to me, and I knew. Shawn and I weren't ready to terminate. If there was something, anything I could do for my family, I was going to do it.

When my MFM doctor returned, we told her our decision that I was going home and going to wait out labor. She strongly advised against it but understood. She told us that West Penn Hospital has a tertiary NICU, and if, by some miracle, I made it to 23 weeks when babies were considered viable, I would go into the hospital at that time and stay on bed rest until the babies arrived. However, if my stomach became sore, any discolored discharge or spiked a fever of any kind, I needed to be rushed back to the hospital immediately because that would indicate an infection that could also endanger my life. So, we went home.

Chapter 5

When we left the hospital, we were both exhausted and utterly starving. I remember stopping at the local Denny's to get some food and to figure out just what the hell we were going to do. We sat over by the large picture window in the front of the dining area, and I decided to call my boss at the time to let her know what had happened. Per my doctor, I needed to rest, not put a lot of stress on myself and limit activities. I didn't have the time to take off work and I didn't know if I qualified for short-term disability, so this was a very anxious phone call. Thankfully, she was so kind and understanding and allowed me to continue working from home so that I wouldn't go insane.

My parents were in Las Vegas that weekend, and I didn't want to call them during their trip and ruin their vacation, so I held off. Shawn called his mom when we got home to give his parents the update, and I could hear the broken voices across the room. I called Cheyan next. Incidentally, Cheyan was also pregnant, and we were originally due the same day, August 10th. How many times in life do best friends truly get pregnant together and yet have the same due date!?

Cheyan has such a big heart and the amount of empathy she feels for others is remarkable, which is why I was terrified to tell her because I knew the stress this would put on her and her pregnancy. But I also knew that if I didn't tell her right away, it would have caused more stress when she did find out. I felt her heart break as the words slowly came out of my mouth, but I knew she would fight this with me as my best friend and as a mom.

The following day was Sunday and when my parents got home from their trip, I gave them a call. "Hey, Mom, how was your trip?" I asked her. She replied, "It was good. What are you guys up to?" Then I proceeded to tell her the horror we went through the day before and as any mom would be, in being protective of her child, she was genuinely upset that I didn't call them on their vacation to tell them of the hard time we were going through. I get it, but they hardly traveled up until that point in their lives and I couldn't ruin that trip with a giant mess of uncertainty. My mom flipped me onto speaker phone so my dad could hear what was going on, and they asked if I would like for the president of the LDS church to come say a blessing to keep the 3 of us safe. My mom was from Utah and raised LDS, which stands for a Latter-Day Saint, while my dad was from Pittsburgh and converted years after meeting my mother. When I was younger, I had also been more spiritual and with Shawn being Catholic, this is where we thought God could save us and our unborn children. I told my mom yes to the blessing; we would do anything at this point. A couple of hours later, both of my parents and the president of the local LDS branch came to my house and, as I sat on the living room ottoman, received his blessing. I am, by no means, a cynic, but my faith had already been struggling for a couple of years. But, receiving a blessing was worth a shot, right?

The night before I had called my parents, I tried sleeping. But, every time I laid flat, I felt like my kids were kicking me in the throat and I would feel more fluid leak out from between my legs. I wasn't sure what I needed to do, but things felt a little more stable when I sat up rather than lay down. I knew I would need to stay upright for the duration of my pregnancy with these little boys, whether it was 3 days or 3 months.

Shawn had this big, thick, plush recliner that he adored and happily gave it to me to use as my perch for the next undefined amount of time. I sat upright in that chair day and night to minimize the amount of fluid leaking from the amniotic sac... I worked in that chair. I ate in that chair. And I slept in that chair. Unfortunately, it was February and cold outside, so I wasn't about to risk slipping on some ice to sit in the ice-chilling temperatures, so I also became a hermit. Every time I would stand up to use the bathroom, let the dogs out, or make lunch, I would get a rush of fluid onto the thick pads I had to practically glue to my body 24 hours a day. I had to be careful to keep my lady parts clean, no shaving and absolutely no sex with my husband. Every couple of days, I would have an appointment with either my OB/GYN or my MFM doctor. Once about a year after everything had happened, my gynecologist had told me in my annual visit that each and every morning during that time in my pregnancy, both of my doctors (OB/GYN and MFM) met on a web call to discuss my situation: how I had not gone into labor yet; best treatment plans based on my current progression; and referred to me as a "ticking time bomb." This process had continued for weeks, and when you're pregnant, each and every single day counts.

Proudly and shockingly, I stayed pregnant. I had continued to grow my little humans inside my body without developing a fever and without going into labor for 6 weeks! Personally, I couldn't believe it. I was mentally exhausted from the toll of worrying about each time I would get a rush of fluid when I moved, if my babies were alive between doctor appointments, the amount of testing each week, the bi-weekly appointments, and overall, physically exhausted as I just needed a solid night's sleep in my own bed where I could lay flat. However, at 23 weeks, we had an appointment with the West Penn NICU doctors and to take a tour of their facility. I recall putting on my cutest maternity shirt, cinched at the waist, that read "Love" in rainbow colors. As we walked into that hospital that day, we held our heads high knowing that our babies were now classified as "viable." We were introduced to a tall woman that I'll refer to as Dr. Kay. She was kind but deliberate. She asked us the obvious question, "If you went into labor today, would you want us to do everything we possibly could to save them?" I immediately thought, duh. I haven't gone through all of this for nothing! But I kindly said, "Of course." The next words that she spoke hit me like one of those glass doors that is so clear that you know it's there, but you can't see it coming. And I walked right into it and felt it smack me in the face that day. You don't see it coming, but man, does it hurt when you walk straight into that sucker. Dr. Kay said, "Okay, then you are not leaving this hospital." I think Shawn was hit by that door a little harder than I was.

I was somewhat expecting to be put on bedrest in the hospital very soon, but not without my belongings and not that day. I think Shawn was expecting it in some way, too, but he wasn't ready to have someone else take care of his wife and live apart from one another for an unknown amount of time. He couldn't live in the hospital with me, as he had to work, and we had two dogs at home that he needed to care for. So, Shawn asked, "Can we leave and get her things and come back later?" Dr. Kay said, "Yes, you have a couple of hours. But, be back by 8:00 pm. When you come into the ER, you'll give them your name, and they will take you to your room." Nothing like a medical hotel to get you set up for seclusion, but deep down I was grateful to have nurses and doctors on call if something should happen. I still know that all of this was necessary at the time, but it didn't make it any easier, emotionally.

When we left, we went straight to Wal-Mart. I drove around in one of those motorized handicapped scooters since I couldn't walk much without leaking down my legs. Shawn followed behind me and put a lot of snacks into his shopping cart for my newfound residence. We were told to bring clothes, slippers, games, books, etc.; anything to make it feel more like home and to keep me comfortable since we didn't know how long I would be there. I was only 23 weeks into my pregnancy, which meant I technically had 17 weeks of bed rest to strive for. The floor I would be staying on was intended for pregnant women living in the hospital on bed rest for all kinds of reasons. I could wear my own clothes, work each day remotely from my room, and would even have my own bathroom. After we filled the trunk with microwaveable macaroni and cheese, chips, crackers, body wash, and shampoo, we then headed home to grab the rest of my belongings. Once we packed my clothes, pillows, blankets, books, and laptop, it was time to go back to the hospital.

Shawn and I looked like a couple of teenage girls going to a sleepover when we walked into the hospital that night with pillowcases full of clothes and snacks. Once we were shown to my room, the nurse took my vitals as Shawn started unpacking and making my bed. The nurse gave Shawn an extra pillow so he could stay my first night with me, and then had me get comfortable so she could put an IV port into my arm. She was so warm and welcoming and told me how I must always keep an IV port in my arm while I was there as a "just in case." The "just in case" was if something immediate happened and they needed that

IV right away, but I learned that a location for an IV port is only good for 3-4 days and then they have to change it to a different location. Over the course of the next 6.5 weeks, I had a total of about 11 different IV ports between both arms, wrists, and hands. The ones on the wrist were the worst, especially when you try to do anything like type on a laptop for work.

After our first night in the hospital and being exposed to my new life of being woken up every 4 hours to take vitals, Shawn had to go home and care for the dogs. I sobbed uncontrollably, to be honest. I had cried so hard after he left that I barely had any breath left in me. Everything we had been put through to get pregnant and stay pregnant was trying to say the least, and now I felt like I was being left in a prison. To say that life up until this point had been a complete mind game is an understatement.

There should be a guidebook or pamphlet for these types of situations called "The Many Mazes and Puzzles of Surviving Bedrest" and I would call this Level 1. I knew I was loved and supported, but to go into this situation feeling 95% physically alone, not knowing what was to come at nearly any moment…unimaginable. Don't get me wrong, the nurses, doctors, and even the cleaning staff were all so kind and friendly, but it was so much more than that. Shawn had even done his best to make it to the hospital every single evening for a few hours before he went off to work for his night shift.

The second day in the hospital was when things really picked up and the medical plans drawn out for me started to take shape. An interesting fact, one of many that I learned that I will share with you, is that when a fetus is 23 weeks along and considered viable, you can receive a series of steroid shots in your upper butt cheek to help the babies' lungs develop a bit quicker. However, it will also increase your blood sugar. Therefore, I needed to take a glucose test prior to being given the Corticosteroids, so that the doctor could be careful of my glucose baseline. The steroids are a set of two injections given 24 hours apart, but it is a one-time deal and they can't be given a second time. Once my glucose test was complete, I was able to start the steroids. Subsequently, I was diagnosed with severe gestational diabetes prior to receiving the steroids. Honestly, I was only 23 weeks along and the ever-so-disgusting sugar test hadn't been a priority while I was sitting with my legs permanently glued shut for survival and never did the outpatient glucose test. The doctor making rounds had started me on quite a bit of insulin; I had 2 short-acting shots and 2 long-acting shots per day. Plus, the 4 sugar checks after every meal and when I would first wake up. It's safe to say that I was the definition of a pin cushion. If you look it up on the web, you will see my picture right next to the phrase "Human Pin Cushion Prisoner."

That was a double-edged sword with my newly diagnosed gestational diabetes. However, I would have consumed a gallon of pure white cane sugar using chopsticks every day if I had thought it would have kept my babies safe. For the record, it doesn't. I was given both shots and would pray that their lungs would develop just enough so that if they had to deliver, they could breathe. Another interesting fact is that the amniotic fluid surrounding a fetus is what they swallow to help their lungs grow and develop properly, the same fluid that my babies were losing each time I moved.

I also had to undergo a non-stress test every single day. Not just any non-stress test, but I would lay at an angle and the nurses would strap two monitors onto my belly to pick up the boy's heartbeats to determine any signs of distress. This should usually only take roughly 30-45 minutes, but when you have two crammed little boys in your stomach that like to kick each other in the heads, it lasts about three hours…every single day. This was my daily routine:

7:00 am: Wake up and shower.

7:30 am: Sign on to the computer to work and answer emails. A nurse would come to take my first blood sugar.

8:00 am: Eat a very bland, no-sugar-added breakfast with a Glucerna shake. Usually eggs and sausage, no ketchup allowed.

9:00 am: A nurse would come and take my next blood sugar and administer insulin.

12:00 pm: Lunch. Usually also bland.

1:00 pm: A nurse would come and take my next blood sugar and administer insulin.

1:30 pm-3:00/4:00 pm: Non-stress test while watching The Food Network on TV or listening to a meeting on my laptop for work.

5:00/6:00 pm: Dinner. Usually still bland.

7:00 pm: A nurse would come and take my next blood sugar and administer insulin.

8:00 pm: Shawn would come to visit me on his way to work.

9:00 pm: A nurse would administer my last shot of insulin for the day.

9:45 pm: Shawn would leave for work, and I would cry until I fell asleep.

When I say this was my routine for weeks, I mean it. The non-stress tests were stressful, as the boys would move or kick off the monitor, a heartbeat would dip, or they weren't in the right position. I also had an ultrasound twice a week, during which the techs would focus on the fluid around each baby and if they were practicing breathing or hiccups. Since my water broke, both babies continuously had low fluid, but they couldn't pinpoint where the tear was. The entire time in the hospital, I continued to have my hospital bed in an upright position to slow as much drainage as possible. My theory was that the tear had to be up higher since I didn't leak as much sitting as when I did laying down. Neither of the babies had ever shown signs of hiccups, but we did see each of them practice small breaths and each second that I got to see that, my heart grew significantly. I was doing something right; this all isn't for nothing.

I was allowed outside occasionally as there was a small park across the street with benches, but other than that, I was in my 4 walls with windows that didn't open. This was Level 2 of the mind game...not just being away from everyone but feeling isolated and not feeling the sun on my face or the wind blow through my hair. Shawn would make it to see me every night around 7:30 pm and stay till about 9:30 pm when he would have to leave for work. On his days off, he would spend most of the day there with me, but it made it even harder to be alone when he left. My older sister would stop in to see me every other week. My parents came to check on me twice. Cheyan and Evan stopped by with dinner a couple of times, and my mother-in-law would stop by every Friday after work. The company helped ease some of the loneliness and made it more bearable.

Since the hospital was limiting my food intake due to gestational diabetes, the one thing I craved the most while pregnant was milk. When you are told, you want things you don't normally like when pregnant, milk was mine. Since milk contains sugar, I couldn't have anything above skim milk and that didn't cut it. Truly, one of my favorite memories of my mother-in-law was that during that time she would sneak me in a bottle of 2% milk every Friday in her purse. It was usually warm and often undrinkable, but the fact that she did that for me spoke volumes.

Level 3 on the mind game was absolutely the worst part, facing reality. A couple of days after I had entered the hospital, the NICU doctor, who we will call Dr. Elle, came to my room to discuss the pregnancy and the babies. This man was older, kind, honest, knowledgeable, and you could tell he had a love/hate relationship with his job. Dr.

Elle began to tell me that due to a broken water at 17 weeks, if the babies were delivered now at 23 weeks+, they would have a very slim chance of surviving. The fluid in the amniotic sac now contains mostly urine from the babies, which provides several protective functions. The first he described was how a baby swallows that fluid to help protect their lungs, helps them develop, and helps their digestive system develop appropriately. Since neither of my boys had enough fluid to develop their respiratory or digestive systems for the last 6+ weeks, chances of life are minimal. I felt like I had been slapped in the face!

He continued to stress that every single day in the womb gives them a slightly greater chance of surviving. Dr. Elle stressed that no matter how far I make it, I need to be prepared for the worst and do my best to get to 28+ weeks. I made it this far; I knew I could get another 5 weeks. Every few days, another NICU doctor on rotation would stop by to discuss the growth and the reality that my children might not live. This was significantly hard on Shawn because he couldn't be with me 24/7 to console me or support me through these tough conversations and had to hear everything secondhand. This is how the weeks went: morning, evening, and night in a continuous terrifying loop and always on high alert.

Chapter 6

When you watch TV or a movie and you see a woman go into labor, there is usually some hilarious panic brought on by the husband as a comedic relief to a serious situation. Then, there is a heartwarming story of getting to the hospital and delivering your gorgeous baby with your family around you. This beautiful screaming infant comes out of your vagina like a prize-winning pig, with everyone being awestruck. Ladies, this is only in movies. Even if I didn't have complications, this would not happen because it's gross, messy, and painful as hell.

Well, I am proud to say that I did not make it to 28 weeks. I made it to 29 weeks and 4 days, which is a huge accomplishment! This meant that I stayed pregnant, kept my boys alive, and survived this mental torture for 12 and a half weeks... with broken water! That is medically unheard of or typically allowed. After going through my 6 weeks of bed rest at home in my husband's recliner and 6 weeks, plus 4 days, of bed rest in the hospital, I began to feel a weird pain like when you pull a muscle in your stomach. The entire time I was in the hospital, I never once rang for the nurse to help me get up, reheat my food (my neighbor two doors down did this often), complain, ask about medications, nothing...I was an ideal prisoner. So, on the night of May 28th, 2017, it was around 7:00 pm and I started to feel very uncomfortable. It was this pain that started up around my ribs and then radiated down around my lower spine. I shifted, thinking it was the two humans inside my body and tried to ignore it until about 7:45 pm when it became a very intense and constant. The moment I hit that red nurse's button on the controller attached to my bed, I knew something was about to happen. Since I had never hit that button in the 6.5 weeks I was living there, the moment I did, two nurses came rushing into my room with a computer on wheels. I honestly do not remember what they looked like except for the panicked expressions, and I have no idea what their names were; the next few hours were a complete blur.

Both nurses began attaching the two straps with heart monitors to my stomach and a monitor for contractions. At this point, it was close to 8:00 pm and I knew Shawn was running a little late but was on his way to the hospital. I didn't know how fast things would be moving or if I was going into labor, so I called him immediately. I remember him answering the phone in the usual way of, "Hey babe, what's up?" He was probably thinking that I was calling him to ask him to smuggle me in another McDonald's cheeseburger on his way, but instead, I asked him where he was. "Hey baby, are you on your way?" I asked him as calmly as I could. He said, "Yeah, I'm almost there, coming down Friendship Avenue now. Are you okay?" No, I wasn't okay. I was terrified. My MFM doctor, OB/GYN, and all of the NICU doctors I had spoken with over the last 3 months had told me that I was high risk and that when things turned, it could be very bad and it would be very quick. I had been reminded several times that a woman shouldn't go longer than 24 hours with a broken water due to infection, and if at any point I had a fever or pain, they were taking the babies whether they were viable or not because it's then risking my life. I was also reminded on multiple occasions that when I went into labor, the babies would be quite fragile, and I would quickly undergo a cesarian section so as not to put any stress on them. Depending on their size, I would either be cut straight down my stomach or through my lower abdomen.

I didn't know what was happening, but thinking of all these warnings, I just needed him to get there. I told him, "I might be in labor. Remember how they said when things turn, it could be quick? I need you to get here. If they take me back soon, you won't be able to come in." There was a lot of commotion going on with nurses coming in and out to check on me, then the on-call OB, and a few other people in scrubs that probably could have been the window cleaning crew. But I did know the pain was getting worse, the machine wasn't picking up contractions, and I needed Shawn. Within minutes, this man of mine came busting into the room in his work clothes, all sweaty and out of breath from parking in the lot down the road and running as fast as he could up the street and through the hospital to get to me. He always shows up. When he came over to me, he had a look of excitement and joy on his face that we were going to meet our little boys.

Shawn was sitting in a chair to my right side and holding my hand tightly as the pain was getting worse. Over the next couple of hours, I was being monitored consistently for contractions. The doctor had prescribed a magnesium drip to help slow preterm labor and reduce the risk of brain bleeds in premature babies. As I lay there while they tried to figure out what was happening, it began to feel like my vagina was on fire and my uterus was going to cause my body to crack open at every joint. Around 11:00 pm, the nurse bent over and took my temperature; it was 100.4. Not exactly a fever. I asked if it could be due to the labor pain I thought I was having, but the nurse said that wasn't likely.

The OB then had me lower my bed and lay flat, which I hadn't done for months. Between the pain of my muscles around my lower back and hips that had shortened from sitting up constantly and the burning volcanic pain coming from my body, I was screaming. Something was wrong, but I had a feeling that this was not what labor was supposed to feel like. When the OB reached her hands up to feel my cervix, I almost kicked her right in the teeth. She confirmed that I wasn't dilating, which they could already tell from the contraction monitor hooked up to help time the waves of when I should start breathing in my nose and out of my mouth. The nurse with the thermometer came back over and took my temperature again; it was 101.2. I had a fever. I was in significant pain. I had an infection, and it was moving fast. I realized I was holding my breath and couldn't breathe. The air in the room became so thick that I felt 100 pounds heavier. I was getting light headed and dizzy. The doctor made the call right then that they needed to get the boys out immediately and directed the nurses to call the NICU to prep.

I had made it to 29 weeks and 4 days. Surely, I had done something right. They were being born and going to be taken care of in their warm incubators while mommy fought this infection. I was completely and utterly proud to take on that burden so that my little boys didn't have to. It was my body, after all, my uterus with this infection, my fever. I don't recall the exact time that I was being prepped for surgery, but I called my parents on their Memorial Day camping trip to let them know I was being taken in for a c-section. My mom answered the phone, wished us good luck, and told me that they would come to see us in the morning. I kissed Shawn, and they began to roll me back to the OR. I remember the operating room like it was yesterday…it was cold, so very cold. I'm not sure why all ORs must be so damn cold. There was a pale green counter to the left with lots of equipment, screens, and lights hovering over the table, and in the back of the room were two giant lights. The lights were on and attached to plexiglass. Below them were two small bassinets on wheels under heat lamps with lots of tools...these were for our babies that I had fought so long and so hard for. I was in shock looking around the room, almost paralyzed. But I was also shivering from the temperature, my anxiety, my fear, and my pain. The table they had me lay on was maybe a foot wide and was quite difficult to balance on. The anesthesiologist wanted to get my epidural in right away, had me bend over, and put that sucker right into my spine. Relief.

That was the first moment of clarity where I could take a deep breath. As he helped me lay backwards and balance my hugely pregnant body on this plank, I started to have a panic attack. He spoke to me to help ground me and talked me through everything the others were doing around me, including why they were strapping my arms down. It reminded me of everything I had gone through, and now I was being sacrificed with my body tied to this thin board as they cut my body wide open.

The doctor was ready to begin when I realized Shawn wasn't in the room yet; it had all happened so fast. A nurse went to get him, and he came in and put that warm, strong arm around my head and talked me through it. We were advised that when a uterus becomes infected, they can get it out in under a minute as it can be life-threatening, but since there are two babies, they'd move as fast as they could.

In the next moment. Screaming. Beautiful, strong, loud, newborn screaming. There was another sound...more screaming from a second newborn. I will never forget hearing those two high-pitched cries. It is one of the most cherished memories of my entire life. Lucas Adam was born at 1:41 am weighing 3lb 5oz, and Colt Michael was born at 1:44 am weighing 2lb 9oz on May 29th, 2017. Shawn's arms were tight around me, and we both began to cry and laugh. I said to Shawn, "They're crying, their lungs are okay!" And Shawn smiled so proudly and kissed me. The boys were placed right into their bassinets on wheels so that they could be taken straight down to the NICU to be stabilized and ready to thrive. On the way out, they stopped each bassinet one at a time so that we could see each of our tiny, beautiful babies. So much relief washed over me when I saw them being rolled away; they were in excellent hands.

If you've never had a c-section, they are truly wonderous procedures. I've heard people comment that c-sections are "the easy way out" of labor, which is a bunch of bullshit. When you're in labor, yes you push, and your vagina can tear as you are pushing a watermelon out. However, two stitches later and some ice, you're back to normal. A c-section is the worst of the two. In a c-section, they have to not just cut through all of thelayers through your hypodermis, but then they have to cut through your physical stomach muscles and move a few organs around before cutting into your uterus to pull out the watermelon and all of its vines. When they're done, they sew up your uterus, put your organs back, and stitch up your gaping wound. When you're in labor and having contractions, those contractions help your body to also know that this pregnancy is finished, and the hormones can slow down.

However, a c-section gives no warning to your body to stop producing those hormones, and once it's cut off abruptly, pun intended, your body goes into this convulsive, uncontrollable shaking. I'm not talking a little hand tremor but shaking so badly that you look like you're having an epileptic episode and could potentially bite your own bottom lip off.

Almost immediately after the boys were rolled away, I began to have these convulsive jerks. I started to panic a little because I couldn't stop, no matter how hard I tried. A nurse escorted Shawn out of the room so that they could stitch me up and wrap me in some blankets. The anesthesiologist reassured me that the shaking was normal due to the hormones, and right then, I told him I felt nauseous. As he reached to grab a bucket, I projectile vomited partway in the bucket, but mostly on him and the floor. I felt terrible, but he didn't even flinch and continued to stand there with the bucket in case it happened again. A few moments later, I was moved to a bed and wheeled into a small area where Shawn was sitting down by my feet. I still couldn't feel anything from my waist down, which was a very unsettling feeling. The nurse who wheeled me down to the OR came in and apologized for what she was about to do. Apparently, after you have a baby, the uterus is supposed to tighten back up quickly, so this means someone must use their backs to push into your abdomen and belly button to shove this organ back down to size. It hurts like hell, but the amount of blood that shoots out from down below is more shocking. Since Shawn had the great luck to sit by my feet, he got to witness all of the bad parts of this process. That was the first time I had ever seen his face turn comically distorted and an odd shade of yellow as he asked, "Is that normal?"

Once I was cleaned up and could start to feel my legs, I was told they were going to wheel me into the NICU to see both babies and then back to my room. To get into the NICU, there was a large, locked metal door that you had to ring a buzzer to get let in. It was about 4:30 am once I was ready to see my boys…it was calm with dimly lit halls, and as you made your way down the corridor, there was a large desk to your left where the nurses sat and a small office-like room behind it for the doctors. Next, were two large metal wash tub sinks. On the right were large glass windows that went from the floor to the ceiling, which continued all the way to the back of the NICU. There were 5 rooms altogether, which they called pods. Each pod could hold up to 6 babies, depending on their severity of care. Since Colt and Lucas were both so small and fragile, they were split into two different pods. I was rolled in Pod 4 first, where I got to see Colt. The next was Pod 5, where I got to see Lucas. Neither of them looked as I had imagined them with the bright pink hue and chubby rolls. Both of my boys were pale white, their veins were visible in every inch of their tiny bodies, you could see the outlines of their ribs and sternum, but the view of their faces were obstructed by wires and tape. It wasn't what I had expected, but they were here, and I was exhausted.

It was around 5:00 am when my hospital bed was rolled back up to my room. From the months of the unknown and the stress, then the last several hours of pain and surgery I had just endured, I was ready to sleep. Shawn wanted to go home and change out of his work clothes that he was still in, so I decided to close my eyes for a bit while he was gone.

Chapter 7

Of all the dates and times that I remember, I do not remember the exact time the nurse woke me up, but it was just after 7:00 am. I had fallen asleep not too long beforehand, but I recognized the nurse as one of the ones that came rushing in the night before when I had pushed the call button. She was older, thin, medium-length, straight gray hair with bangs and glasses. She cautiously shook me, and when I looked up at her, her face said it all. I was startled and slid my head back, dazed, when then I heard the most terrifying 3 words slip out of her mouth with a sense of urgency, "The NICU called." Okay, I questioned, are they giving an update? Are they checking on me? I just saw my kids not that long ago, and they were both asleep in their little incubators. I knew she could tell the confusion on my face as she started again, "The NICU called, and they need to see you." That heart-wrenching feeling alarmed me that I was about to enter the next level of this never-ending race, and there were no cheat codes or magic wizards to get us through.

Immediately, I tried to stand up, but with the epidural still wearing off and having my stomach muscles cut open, I fell backward onto the bed. When the nurse came in to wake me up, she had come prepared with the wheelchair, which she then moved closer to the bed and had me lock my fingers around her neck so she could help me up and we could move together. I stood up, and we pivoted until the back of my legs hit the chair, and then I sat down. She pulled one of my blankets off my bed and covered my lap. She pushed me down the hall, inside the elevator, and back to the large metal door. Once they buzzed us in, a blonde-haired nurse with black-rimmed glasses and bright blue scrubs was waiting for me. She thanked my nurse and bent down to my eye level to talk to me. She asked how I was feeling, and that Dr. Elle needed to see me in Pod 5. Pod 5 was Lucas' incubator…shit. Tears started pouring down my face as they wheeled me between the two sliding glass doors. There were almost a half dozen doctors and nurses surrounding my son's bed with masks and gloves on, some talking loudly while others were hushed. The lights were on to full capacity, and the beeping sounds of the monitors were constant. I stared at this scene in horror. My heart was breaking because I knew exactly why I had been brought here. I looked around at the other 5 incubators that had brightly colored fleece blankets over them to block the lights from bothering the infants, and no other parents were allowed with their children while the doctors worked to save my son's life.

Dr. Elle was sitting on a high stool to my left with a computer directly in front of him; his gray hair around his head was a bit unruly, and his glasses were at the tip of his nose. He looked like he was also running a marathon. He spoke directly to me in his honest, caring voice, and I began shaking. I sat there in my wheelchair listening to Dr. Elle as the blond-haired nurse in blue scrubs kneeled at my right side with her hands holding mine. Dr. Elle said very clearly, "Your son is not saturating; we've been trying, but it doesn't look good." What…what did he mean by saturating? I couldn't speak to ask, but thankfully, he continued to explain. Saturating is when your blood is taking enough oxygen to your lungs so you can breathe. Saturation levels need to be above 90-92 for a newborn. They had him on a ventilator to push more oxygen into his little body and connected him to an oscillator, which manually shakes the body to help the lungs move in and out. Even with this help, they couldn't even register his saturation levels.

I was in shock. I didn't know what to say or do, but I begged him…I remember screaming as though I had been punched in the stomach and begged him to save my son's life as I bent over sobbing. Dr. Elle turned bright pink, and I heard the choke in his throat when he told the nurse to take me back up to my room so I could call my husband, and they would keep doing their best. Writing this down and bringing those visuals back into my mind is so difficult; it's hard to continue writing even with a couple of breaks to walk away. But, taking the time to process that this truly happened, the sight I saw with all of those doctors and the chimes and alarms going off on the monitors brought my son back to life for a few moments because he was real. He is real.

The nurse in blue scrubs took me back to my room; I refused to get back in my bed. There was no use since I wasn't going to be here long, I needed to be back down in that NICU with my baby. I called Shawn, who was oblivious to what was happening because the last time I had seen or spoken to him, our children were safe. I remember crying and not being able to form the words and hearing him get upset because he needed to know what was happening. All I said was, "You need to get back here; it's Lucas." We hung up, and I anxiously waited for him to walk back through that door. I had started to calm down and breathe again, but when I saw him, it was like my soul collapsed. I tried explaining to him what I saw and what they told me, but I couldn't get the words out. He grabbed the handles of my chair, and we went back downstairs. This time, when we were buzzed through the doors, only one doctor was standing over Lucas's incubator and the kind nurse in blue scrubs was beside him. Shawn pushed me up to the incubator so that I could peer inside, and there was my gorgeous little boy. He was still very pale, with purple veins showing through his thin layer of skin and what seemed to be 100 wires attached to him in all different directions. The numbers on the screen were still flashing, but you could see they had put the alarms on silent. But why were they silent if it was still going off? They needed to know he was still in danger. But they knew.

The doctor at his incubator was Dr. G, an older man with a very empathetic face and a slight accent. Shawn was pushed up against the plastic of the incubator, looking down at his son's little body, when Dr. G said that they had tried everything and would give it a couple of hours to see if anything changed. He allowed us to put our hands in the incubator and touch him very carefully,but advised us not move our hands back and forth. The nurse explained that when babies are born so early, their nerves are exposed on their skin, and rubbing our hands over his head or stomach could be painful, so we had to set our hands on him gently. I knew what this meant, the fact that they were letting us touch him while his monitors continued to silently chime. When we did our NICU tour, the doctor told us that we aren't generally allowed to touch a preemie for the first week of life because of the frailty; the first week is when they are at the highest risk of brain bleeds.

I don't think my heart and head spoke to each other at all after that. I have never, in my life, seen so much fear in my husband's face or felt his hand so tight on mine. The fear of losing his son, losing his dream of identical twin boys, and the fear of what this would do to his wife and his family. For not being particularly practicing religious people, we prayed like hell and prayed through the tears. Shawn begged God to take him instead and asked the doctors repeatedly to take his lungs to save Lucas. I sobbed at the reality that no matter how hard I tried and everything I had done, somehow, I felt like I had failed my son. I failed my husband. I failed my family. The guilt rushed over me that it was my fault that our son was dying in front of us, and Shawn was losing one of his boys. After who knows how long we were sitting there in tearful silence, the blonde-haired nurse came in to tell us that my parents were there. Shit, I forgot to call them.

With all of this happening, we never thought of calling our families. She asked if we wanted them to be with us. We said yes, so she called back up to my room to tell the nurses where to send them. She met them in the hallway, and my mom came rushing through those closed glass doors into Pod 5 like only a mother could. When she turned the corner, she saw me sitting in my wheelchair with my hand on my son's head in complete silence. She sat next to me with her arm around my shoulder as I began to sob, "He's going to die." She put her other arm around my head and brought it to her shoulder. There is something magical about a mother's hug, the reassurance of strength. We sat there like that while Shawn explained the situation to my dad and older sister, Heather. The 3 of them had come to see their new family members and brought a beautiful bouquet of flowers, not knowing the hell they were walking into. Not long after, my mother-in-law arrived, who we also forgot to call back. The 6 of us sat around this small boy with so much love, so much hope, so much sadness that it was felt in our bones.

It was about 2:00 pm when Dr. G came back in and told us to go back to my room to take a break and come back down in an hour. He also suggested to call one of our churches to have someone baptize him. The blonde-haired nurse offered to call her church, and we agreed.

When we went back upstairs, Shawn's sister, Tina, and her boyfriend were waiting for us. Most of the family waited in the hallway as I crawled back into my bed and struggled to breathe through the tears. When my nurse came in to check on me, I refused any pain medication. There was no way I deserved any relief from this pain; if my baby was suffering, then so was I. Shawn and my dad tried to talk me into taking an Ibuprofen since I just had my body cut open, but no way. This pain was justified; I hadn't saved my babies after all.

My mom stood next to my right side, never letting go of my hand while my dad paced the room. My mother-in-law rocked back and forth quietly while my sister and Shawn's sister stood in the hallway talking. Right before 3:00 pm, we were all breathing again when Shawn said he was going back down to check to see what was happening. I was calm. I had this odd feeling of calmness, probably from all the hormones my body was releasing from the pregnancy and the tears I had shed. I was in pain, but I had that high feeling from being overtired.

I stared at the clock, waiting for him to come back, and when he did, I felt every piece of my body break into a million pieces. He walked into the room with a straight face and said, "They need just you and me. It's time," and with that, he walked into the bathroom near my bed and locked the door. I didn't recognize the voice coming from my mouth except for the blood-curdling scream and kicking my feet as each of my parents held my hands. I repeated over and over, "I swear I would make a good mom. I swear I would make a good mom." My parents squeezed my hands tightly while tears rolled down their faces, and then my dad realized Shawn locked himself in the bathroom. He started knocking continuously on the bathroom door to get Shawn to answer to make sure he was okay, which he wasn't, of course. He opened the door, and his eyes were bright red with snot coming down his face. He and my dad helped me back into that wheelchair as our families waited in the room. As we rolled out of my room, my sister and sister-in-law were standing there with soaking faces. I was afraid to look them in the eyes, so I looked at the floor not wanting to feel any pity and feeling ashamed.

Going back through those doors and into Pod 5, Dr. G was there waiting for us to tell us there was nothing else they could do. Our son couldn't bring any oxygen into his body; therefore, his brain and body had suffered significantly. They asked if we had any clothes that we wanted him to wear and that the priest from the nurse's church was there. Before the nurse changed him into his little blue monster outfit and hat, the priest came in to say a prayer and baptize Lucas. We asked if he could please also baptize Colt while he was there. I hate to say it, but so much was demanded from us that morning and afternoon for Lucas that we hadn't thought much about Colt's well-being. We figured he was doing okay since no one was rushing to his side, and right now, Lucas needed us more. I guess that a part of parenting is sometimes one child may need you more than the other and vice versa. As a mother or father, for that matter, you learn how to balance those needs and do your best to make sure all of your children are supported, especially in their time of need.

After the baptism, Lucas was changed, and Shawn asked if we could put our sons together one last time. Lucas' little body was placed into my arms, and we were wheeled back into Pod 4 to Colt's incubator. We looked up at his monitors; he was saturating oxygen, but barely. His alarms would chime every other minute when there was a dip and then come back up and dip again. The nurse lifted Lucas from my arms, put him facing Colt, and turned Colt to face Lucas. Shawn lost it, tears flooding the room again. When you ask Shawn and I if we've ever witnessed a miracle, we will both say yes. We later found out that every doctor in that NICU that day thought we were going to lose Colt too, but when we put them together in that incubator, we witnessed a true miracle. Lucas subtly moved his hand out and touched Colt's hand, and within seconds, we saw Colt's oxygen saturation rise, his heart rate slowed, and his respirations temporarily steadied. It was as though our sweet little Lucas was telling his little brother goodbye and that he loved him, all while knowing that we needed Colt to survive and told him to fight because he no longer could. I'm not sure how long we stayed like that, but we were able to get a couple of pictures of our identical twin boys together. The sun was lower outside the slitted shades when I told Colt that we would be back in a little while and rolled out of Pod 4 with Lucas in my arms.

In the back hallway was a small room used for grieving families, which is heartbreaking knowing that there was even a need for that room or how often it is used. Inside the tiny room, to the right were two chairs with a small table in between and a small walkway to the left to get to the sink on the back wall. Shawn sat in the chair to the far back while my wheelchair was rolled next to him and turned around to face the door. We then had to say our goodbyes. I cannot write this without sobbing, and as I sit here, let me tell the truth. There is no such thing as telling your child goodbye. Your child that you fought for, that you loved so absolutely, that it was your job to keep safe. We could have been told 5 years before we had children that this would happen and to start grief counseling, and we still wouldn't have been ready. We sat in that room for at least an hour crying and taking turns apologizing and saying goodbye to our baby when Dr. G walked in. He bent down and listened to Lucas' heart while he was laying on Shawn's chest, and gave the nod that our baby was gone. Our baby was gone. My son, who I was only able to hear cry one single time was now gone.

The room felt stale, like the air couldn't circulate, and started to strangle both of us. Shawn held onto that tiny little boy on his chest that he dreamed of being a dad to and wept uncontrollably. I lowered my head, tears pouring down my face, and screamed while the nurse came rushing in to hold my head to her chest. At this moment, there was no consoling as Shawn and I were very reactive to this situation, and neither could navigate this. We were distraught, we were angry. We sat in that room until our eyes were dry; we were both out of breath, our throats sore from screaming, our eyelids weighed about twenty pounds, and neither of us spoke to each other.

Once we were calmer, my mom and older sister came into the room for grieving families, and the nurse brought in three more chairs. My mom sat down in a chair against the wall and held her grandson for the first and only time as pain settled onto her face and tears poured down her cheeks. My sister went to find my dad, as he had gone for a walk and needed air after the day from hell that they didn't expect. Once she found him, he came rushing into the room. One thing to know about my dad is how absolutely he loves his children and grandchildren; he would truly do anything, including volunteering to lose a limb to make any piece of their lives better. I knew this would be difficult on him, and when he sat next to my mom, it was pure despair for this tough man as he also held his grandson for the one and only time.

Heather stood behind my chair, and every now and then, I would feel her touch my shoulder, which I think she was doing to let me know she was present and there, but she didn't know how to maneuver the situation either and would get choked up and remove her hand. Shawn's mom and sister came into the room next to hold Lucas and give him their love. It was traumatic watching all the people I cared for say goodbye to their grandson and nephew. Sometime around this point, one of the nurses from my room upstairs came into the room to check on me and had two small white paper cups in her hand. She bent down next to my right leg and looked up at me with warmth to remind me that I hadn't had any pain medication that day and hadn't eaten or had any water. In one of the cups was pain medication and the other cup had some water in it, both of which I rejected. I know now that she was being kind and doing her job, which was to take care of her patient. But I was bitter, solemn, and angry. I snapped at her and told her no; I didn't want either of them. Everyone in that tiny room, all 8 people, gently spoke to me and asked me to take some pain medication as I had just recently had my stomach muscles separated from my body. I refused both cups again; I was not taking this pain away that I felt I deserved. I was so raw. My son was gone, and the physical pain I felt couldn't compare to the broken soul I now had. Everything in my body felt broken, all the way down to my cells; nothing else mattered. It was late when Dr. G came into the room, which didn't have any windows, and asked if they could take Lucas back so that we could go up to my room and rest. He offered to put a privacy screen around Colt's incubator and allow Lucas to lay in a bassinet next to his incubator until morning. At first, Shawn and I hesitated, but I could see the fatigue on Shawn's face, so we both agreed to go back upstairs for a bit, but we would be back to be with our boys. Once we made it upstairs and I finally crawled back into my bed, our families gave us their hugs and went home as everyone needed a break.

From living upright for the previous 12.5 weeks, my body couldn't lay straight on a bed without a great amount of pain in my lower back and hips. I lifted the back of the bed and laid there quietly, upright, without any sound and stared up at the ceiling tiles. I needed the room to be quiet, and so did Shawn. He laid back in the chair next to my bed; his whole body collapsed as his brain shut down, and he closed his eyes for some rest. It wasn't voluntary rest, but his mind and body literally shut down.

I later found out that during the day, Heather had been texting with Cheyan, who I hadn't had a second to call and tell her anything that was going on. Heather was supposed to let our dogs out while we were resting and celebrating the birth of our new babies in the hospital, but instead, she stayed with us while we grieved. So, Heather kept Cheyan updated on what was happening and asked her to take care of the dogs.

While Shawn was resting, I thought about calling Cheyan but didn't have the strength to lift my phone or to use the muscles in my face to form words. But, as the greatest friend I could ask for in life, she barreled into that hospital room within minutes of the thought of needing her came into my head. I didn't have to call her; she knew I needed her and came without me asking. As soon as she and Evan came through the door, I lost it again. I didn't think I had anything else left in my body, but she sat on my bed and just hugged me while we both sobbed. Evan sat quietly in the corner, but knowing he was there when Shawn woke up seemed to lift Shawn's spirits a bit as well.

That evening, after the sun had gone down, the nurses on the floor kept checking in on me and Shawn more than they usually were. The truth is, we wanted to be alone as we both felt numb and just needed time for our brains to process what had just happened over the last 24 hours. One of the nurses reminded Shawn and I that while in our vegetative states, that we had another child that we needed to take care of, and we couldn't do that if we didn't take care of ourselves. So, we both ate something and turned Chopped on the TV for something to watch mindlessly. The last thing I remember from that evening before falling asleep is lying on my right-side facing Shawn while he was on his left side. We held hands tightly as I tearfully whispered, "Our son died today." And he painfully whispered back, squeezing my hand, "I know, baby."

Chapter 8

The next morning, I woke up around 6:00 am, the sun was starting to peek through the dark blinds, and when I looked over, Shawn wasn't there. I figured he had gone for a walk or to get some breakfast, but as I pulled the blanket up to disappear back into the bed, knowing that yesterday was real, he walked through the door. I knew that the day was going to be awful again, and I just wanted it to end. I wanted to disappear; I wanted to melt away into nothing and not exist anymore. I cannot explain the sorrow you feel after losing a child, but no parent should ever have to feel that in their bones. It's not like the sadness when you lose a grandparent or when an old friend passes away. There's a physical and emotional piece to this kind of loss. It feels like part of your stomach and heart has been removed from your body, as though organs are physically missing, and there is this hollow feeling deep inside your body.

Then, the emotional part is whether this all was real, and while knowing it was real, you have moments of clarity when you think to yourself that you will be okay, but then you feel like you can no longer survive again. Shawn and I had the unfortunate luck of trying to process this awfulness while trying to be happy and celebrating that Colt was alive and we had a beautiful baby we needed to be there for. We couldn't just drift away into nothingness, but to this day, I do not feel as though we had a chance to properly grieve then, which took its toll on both of us.

Shawn sat quietly next to me, and I asked him where he had been; he told me the NICU. I threw the blankets off me, ready to put on my broken armor and go take care of Colt, but Shawn stopped me and told me to relax because he was down there to see the boys; there wasn't an emergency. I sat back and tried to calm my breath when I realized how badly I needed to pee. This was the next problem; the nurses felt pity on me, so I had used it to my advantage the day before to keep the catheter in place, so I didn't have to move from my chair. However, before falling asleep the night before, they had to remove it to reduce the risk of infection. The issue was that after you have a c-section, you are encouraged to get up and walk around as soon as possible and as much as possible so that your body can heal correctly. Well, I had thrown in that towel the day before and only stood a couple of times to get to my wheelchair and back into bed, but now I had no choice.

Shawn helped me swing my feet off the bed, and when I started to stand up, I felt every muscle from my ribs to my vagina pull and try to tear my torso in half like when you pull a zipper that is stuck on a canvas tent, and it splits at the seams. I sat back down. After I caught my breath, Shawn asked if I wanted the nurse for pain medicine; I said no. I stood back up, determined to get to the bathroom, and that's when the wave of blood from giving birth rushed out of my body. I had no choice now; I had to get to the bathroom. As I made it to the toilet, Shawn lovingly helped me remove my clothes and cleaned me up while I tried stopping him from seeing my broken body. He never said a word as he removed the paper diaper I had been wearing and wiped blood from my legs and feet. Then, he helped me walk back towards my bed, and I sat in the wheelchair so we could go see our babies.

I feel like at this point in our lives, Shawn and I had gone through so much struggle and heartbreak that when most people would turn away from each other, we turned towards each other. We didn't have to speak; we almost read each other's sorrow and were able to ache silently while holding each other's hand to keep us from crumbling. When we walked into Pod 4, there was a large partition wall around Colt's incubator separating the rest of the room from him and Lucas. Lucas was lying in his small bassinet next to his brother's bed, wearing the bright blue and black striped monster outfit we had him dressed in the day before with the matching hat and swaddled tightly in a blanket. I got to hold my son one last time that morning before the doctors told us they had to take him now, as we wouldn't want to see what happens in the next few hours to days. We woefully cried and kissed his sweet little head one last time. They rolled my oldest son away from us while we prayed that our youngest son would survive.

We were stuck in a weird limbo of grief and sorrow of losing Lucas and then trying to be positive and find the light in each day as Colt fought his damnedest. We learned the hard way that there is no appropriate or inappropriate way to grieve. Grief is something that is so objective but concrete that it's almost tangible. Most of us, if not all, have experienced grief, whether over the loss of a family member, a friend, a pet, or even the loss of a job or a breakup. How our bodies and minds respond to that loss differs greatly from one person to the next. We saw several parents and grandparents lose their little ones that week; it was almost as if a dark cloud had fallen over the NICU. The nurses and doctors were ragged; there was no peace of mind to be found, plenty of alarms chiming, tears falling from one end to the other of that ward, and hope was in little supply. Each person's face, from doctor to parent, looked as though we had been fighting a battle in this war. Shawn and I were lost, not knowing what was "appropriate" to feel or say or do as all we could do now was watch this tiny 2lb 9oz little boy breathe through a machine and have his whole body shaken to help his lungs move. That's when we met Debbie; she was one of the NICU nurses that left a lasting impression.

Debbie was a little older; she was thin with short brown hair and had the sweetest, calming voice I had ever heard. Shawn and I were both drawn to her, as though she was an angel there to help us, and when she spoke, we listened. Shawn and I started taking the next couple of days hour by hour, per her advice. Go to my room, get some rest, come back down, repeat. Debbie took the time to explain to us how the patient-to-nurse ratio worked depending on the criticalness of the infant. If there was an infant like ours that was critical, there was a 1:1 nurse ratio per patient. Or if the infants in that pod weren't as critical, the nurse-to-infant ratio may be 1:2 or 1:3. Debbie also asked if she could be a primary nurse for Colt so that when she was on shift, she would always have him as her patient, if possible. Debbie gave us the two greatest pieces of advice a parent could receive while having a child in critical care. First, you are your child's best advocate. While the doctors and nurses are there to care for your baby, they rotate every shifts and change each day, but you are the one consistent factor in your baby's life, and if something seems off, advocate. Speak up and speak up again until you know what is going on and your baby is cared for. Secondly, she also told us to write down everything we were about to go through in a notebook so that we would have all of Colt's milestones written down, and I am so grateful that we did. Hence, this book.

On May 31st, just two days after the twins were born, Colt's oxygen began to decline again. All the nurses and doctors were truly amazing in that NICU, and each one would take the time to explain every little detail and were patient with all of our questions. Colt's oxygen saturation had reached 70% with 100% pure oxygen, which is dangerously low, and we were worried about brain damage. One of the doctors explained to us that this would be a "one step forward, 3 steps back" battle over the next unknown number of months. We were also told that Colt was on the oscillator to help his lungs move to bring in the oxygen, but they were committed to getting him off pure oxygen and onto blended air as soon as possible. We learned that being on pure oxygen causes retinopathy of prematurity, or ROP, which is when the blood vessels in the eyes don't develop correctly and can curl or stop growing. ROP is most common in babies receiving pure oxygen and who were born earlier than 28 weeks, which we were smack dab in the middle of both. It was also explained to us that Stevie Wonder was born premature and was on pure oxygen, which caused his blindness because the side effects weren't known at the time of his birth. This was terrifying but also very insightful. The more you know....

The doctor explained to us that there are 5 different types of ROP that can cause blindness and need to be monitored over the next couple of months because if it does happen to occur and if caught early enough, there is a treatment by laser eye therapy. This was day 3, and my head was spinning as I tried to write everything down and understand our new reality, but we were both asking every question that we could so that we could learn enough to make the best decisions possible.

On June 1st, I was told that I was being released from the hospital to go home. This was a curse and a blessing all at the same time. I was being sent home after 7 weeks in hospital isolation to go into the world. I was being sent home to sleep in my own bed after 12.5 weeks of living in an upright position. But I was also being sent home without either of my children. I remember clearly how ready Shawn was to get out of there and just take a normal minute to breathe. When my nurse brought in my discharge paperwork, he had everything from a 7 week stay packed up and loaded into a large suitcase, a duffel bag, and several large plastic bags, which he piled onto my lap as I sat in the wheelchair. I froze when it was time to leave. It's genuinely cruel that life happens in such a way that a woman is sent home from the hospital to rest and sleep in the comfort of her own bed while there are strangers caring for her child, who is is alone and struggling to survive. Shawn coaxed me out of that room, though he promised we would be back the next morning, and we would spend the entire day with Colt. I was now officially on maternity leave, and Shawn was on bereavement. It was such a strange concept that I had to use my maternity leave without having a crying baby to get on a sleep schedule or get into a nursing rhythm, but I could use that time to heal mentally and physically.

Deep down, I knew and saw what my husband did that week to protect me; I just stayed quiet and acted like they didn't happen. Because if I ignored it, it was supposed to hurt less, right? Shawn had to file the paperwork for the boy's birth certificates, then a paper for a death certificate, and he began to make arrangements for the funeral. I knew it would be a closed casket if we went that route, but I was praying I could see him one last time. On the way home from the hospital that day, Shawn pulled up to the front door of the funeral home we had chosen, and they brought everything right out to the truck so that neither of us had to walk through those large iron doors. Admittedly, it was one of the kindest gestures I have ever experienced, and I was so thankful. We both had to sign a couple of papers, and I begged the man at the window to let me see my baby again, as they had picked him up from the hospital that morning. We were strongly advised not to, as that is not how we should remember our baby. So, we had chosen to have Lucas cremated because the thought of putting my tiny 3lb 5oz baby in the cold ground was incomprehensible. Shawn had a very specific urn in mind; it was an angel about 14 inches tall with the hands folded in front of the chest and had a stunning iridescent gloss over it that made it shimmer. Once the arrangements were made, we drove home while Shawn held my hand as I sobbed.

On June 2nd, we slept in a little bit and spent some time playing with the dogs before heading to the hospital in the late morning. As we were walking out of the front door to get in the truck, my phone rang and said, "West Penn NICU" across the screen. I had a chocolate ice cream bar sticking out of my mouth as my hands were full of things for Colt's area at the hospital; I froze in the middle of the front yard when I saw who was calling. Shawn had already climbed into the driver's seat and was sitting inside with the door open when he saw my face. I spit the ice cream bar out and answered. The doctor on the other end was not one I was familiar with yet, as they had several different doctors that rotated through. Before I could say anything more than "hello," the deep accented voice on the other end was explaining to me that the high pressure from the ventilator and the oscillator that Colt was on to keep him alive had popped his left lung. I ran to the truck, waving for Shawn to drive as he was yelling at me in his impatient voice, "What?!" I pulled the phone down slightly and said, "The pressure from the ventilator popped Colt's lung." I was then thrown back in my seat as Shawn quickly gained speed.

The doctor's deep voice continued calmly with this thick accent and not so subtle confidence. He explained that this was "quite common" and a "risk factor" of the ventilator, and his plan of treatment would be to insert a temporary chest tube to relieve fluid and air for a couple of days and "it will heal on its own." I firmly replied to his explanation with, "Then why are you talking to me instead of putting in the chest tube?! We are on our way; go do it!" It was later explained to us that while it was needed, it wasn't a medical emergency, or they would have done it right away and called us afterward. We stayed there the rest of the evening until about 10:00 pm, when we both started falling asleep in the large wooden rocking chairs the nurse provided us.

The next couple of days went the same way as we started a routine. We would wake up around 8:00 or 9:00 am. I would pack us a lunch so that we could stay with Colt as long as possible, and then we would leave for the hospital by 10:00 am. We would get to the NICU by 10:45-11:00 am. At this point, we still weren't allowed to hold Colt but were allowed to put our hands in the incubator to rest on his head or stomach. We wanted to be at the hospital each day before 12:00 pm because that is when the doctors would make their rounds through each pod and would meet individually with the parents to give updates and answer any questions.

We had learned that the first 7 days of a premature baby's life are the most critical to prevent bleeding in the brain. What happens is when an infant is born too early or is less than 3.5 lbs, there is a high risk of a brain bleed that starts to diminish after the first 7 days of life. There are different grades of these bleeds that can cause various degrees of damage since their blood vessels are so small and fragile, but it's called an intraventricular hemorrhage (IVH). After the first week of life, they would perform an ultrasound on Colt's head to determine if he had an IVH and what grade it was, which ranged from 1-4. Grades 1 and 2 are mild brain bleeds that we were told usually resolved themselves, meaning that the body would reabsorb the blood and not really cause any damage or any that could be noticed. Grades 3 and 4 are more severe brain bleeds that cause things like developmental delays, cerebral palsy, extra fluid in the brain, and loss of life. When the nurses would rotate Colt to either bathe him or care for him, he was in a small "U" shaped pillow that they would turn him slowly on so they wouldn't jostle him around or bump his head in any way.

After sitting with Colt for a while, we would go across the hall to the family waiting room, eat our lunch, and then go back in and read him stories and talk with the nurses.

After or during every Penguins Hockey game, Shawn would sit close to the incubator to give him a play by play. We would leave the hospital around 5:00 pm and walk around Lawrenceville to get some air and find dinner at a local restaurant. After dinner, we would go back to the hospital until about 10:00 pm, when we would go home to rest and do it all again the next day. This continued for a few weeks until Shawn had to go back to work, but I still had six more weeks on my own to be with my baby. The only change in our routine in those first couple of weeks was Monday, June 5th.

June 5th was the day of Lucas' memorial. Initially, I wanted to keep it small and private, but then I wanted all our friends and family to be able to support us in showing their love for our little angel. Waking up that day and picking out an outfit for your child's funeral is surreal and feels so unimportant. You need and want to find the most appropriate thing to wear, but then you have a conflicting feeling of not giving a shit about what you're going to wear because this is going to be the second worse day of your life. I had chosen black pants, a soft black shirt with lace across the shoulders, a black cardigan, and black slip-on shoes with a small bow on the toes. Shawn and I left our house around 1:00 pm to get to the funeral home. He held my hand as I slowly walked through those doors, still sore from the c-section. We were greeted by the funeral director with a warm hug and a broken smile then directed into our area for the service. Both sets of our parents were there when we arrived and followed behind us without saying much.

The very second that I walked into the room and saw Lucas' shimmering angel urn, I felt that uneasy feeling of being hollow and my brain shutting down as tears poured down my cheeks. I sat in the high-backed chair with a floral print that was placed next to the table. The next few hours were a blur, but one thing that stuck out to me was that my father-in-law had sat next to me in his giant-hearted but protective way the entire time. As people would come up to me, he would listen to what they were saying, and I recall him saying a couple of times to people, "That's enough," and directing them towards the crowd of people sitting in banquet chairs. My next memory of that day is when we were asked to sit up front as the priest would give the service. I laid my head on Shawn's shoulder and bawled uncontrollably as he spoke. I heard the sniffles and muffled cries from our family and friends behind us. This was a nightmare. Everything about it, every face that walked through that door and hugged me, every tear shed in that room, the side looks of people checking on me and looking for my expression, it was one of my lowest points.

After our angel baby's service, we left to go home quickly and change our clothes so we could go be with Colt. When we arrived that evening, the doctor who made the rounds that morning came to speak with us, which was always alarming when they walked into the pod to talk to a parent after rounds. It was Dr. G; he wanted to check on us, knowing the service was earlier that day. He then stood next to Colt's incubator with a handful of papers to tell us what had occurred since we left the night before, as it had been a busy day and we didn't make it for rounds.

Dr. G told us that the night before, they had taken Colt off dopamine to see how he would respond. Colt was on dopamine to help his heart work efficiently and to help keep his blood pressure up, but since he was now a week old, they had stopped it, and his blood pressure was maintaining well on its own. The next change was that they were able to remove Colt's UA line, which is a catheter inserted directly into a baby's umbilical artery that comes from the umbilical cord. The UA line is very delicate, as it is directly in an artery and can only stay in for about a week, but it helps the NICU team deliver medicine directly into their circulation system. It also helps them with taking blood samples without having to keep poking these little humans and increasing the risk of infection. With them being able to remove the UA line, Colt could now be placed on his stomach, which also helps open the lungs to bring in more oxygen.

The next step was that they stopped the antibiotics that they had been giving him for the past week as he was delivered from a uterus that had an infection. He had not only been premature with underdeveloped lungs, but he had also swallowed the infection that was in the fluid in the placenta, and they needed to help his body get rid of the bacteria. Next, Colt's lung had healed itself within a couple of days, and they were even able to remove his chest tube. Dr. G then told us that about an hour before we arrived, they had done the head ultrasound since Colt was officially 7 days old. I was already exhausted from earlier that day, but this made me feel like I had whiplash. He explained to us that they found a grade 1 sub-bleed, which was astonishing given the criticalness of his first week of life. My brain was putting the pieces together. Colt's heart was maintaining blood pressure, he could now be put on his stomach to let his lungs open, the UA line was out, his lung had healed the hole, and the minor brain bleed shouldn't cause any issues as the body would reabsorb the blood. We had finally heard some great news, which we desperately needed! That night was the first decent night of sleep that Shawn and I had in months. We had put our angel baby to rest, and our little survivor rested comfortably with the best care imaginable.

June 6th was a big day for our little family. He was just over a week old now without a UA line and a minor brain bleed. That morning, Colt was taken off the oscillating vent and put on a conventional vent, meaning his lungs would have to do all the work. It was stressful sitting in those chairs watching his oxygen saturation dip up and down, but the doctor explained that if they didn't push him a little bit to make his lungs move on their own, they would get complacent, and it would be harder to do so the longer they waited. All night, Debbie had been able to wean his pure oxygen down to room air, and they were going to extubate him and place him on NPV. NPV stands for negative pressure ventilation, which is where every now and then, there is some additional help from a vent to expand the lungs and then allow the body to exhale on its own.

June 7th was the first time we got to hold our baby. We could only hold him for short amounts of time while he could tolerate our touch and room temperature, which the nurses could measure by his statistics. I was sitting in one of the large wooden rocking chairs when Debbie unhooked one side of the incubator, and the wall fell open. She wrapped our little baby in a couple of warm blankets and put a hat on his head. She slowly moved while holding him still, with all his tubes and cords, and placed him in my arms. Holding my baby for those short 20 minutes that day was the most joy I had experienced since hearing them scream when they were born. Debbie then picked him up and placed him in Shawn's arms, and tears began to fall down his cheeks. This little boy was going to survive; we knew it. When we left that night, we were both elated but also very anxious, worrying that his lungs would fail, or he would go backward as we were warned preemies often do. But when we arrived the next morning, Colt was still on the NPV!

On June 8th, 10 days after Colt was born, the doctors inserted his first feeding tube. There are different types of feeding tubes that we were learning about, and his called a "G-tube." A G-tube is surgically placed directly from the outside of the body into the stomach so that food bypasses the intestines, but the baby starts to get adequate nutrition. During our daily meeting with the NICU doctors, they explained to us the absolute need to provide premature babies with breast milk, as it was the healthiest and safest way to start them on food, or else they could develop necrotizing enterocolitis (NEC). NEC is when premature intestines are damaged or get infected, which can be fatal to the baby. We were able to start giving Colt small amounts of the milk I had been working so hard to pump the past week, but I couldn't keep up with the volume they needed as his daily feedings would quickly increase. Nursing is a difficult task that not all women can or want to do, which is totally fine! I am all for "fed is best." But, knowing this was a life-saving decision for Colt, I was trying every few hours. Unfortunately, no matter how hard I tried and pumped, my hormones wouldn't respond enough to a plastic cup attached to my boobs by a pulsing suction to increase my milk production. So, I signed a waiver to allow the NICU to use donor breast milk to keep my baby thriving. The waiver detailed that the breast milk was treated, so it wasn't 100% the same as it was coming from my body, but it was safe to use.

Chapter 9

The next couple of weeks ran on clockwork as we continued our routine, but then Shawn had to go back to work. With Shawn returning to working night turn and sleeping during the day, I developed some separation anxiety from Colt and was with him almost every waking hour. The new routine would start by 8:00 am, and I would then grab my lunch and leave for the hospital before 9:00 am. Once there, I would sit next to Colt's bed and talk to him like we had been best friends our entire lives and had lived through hell together. I would tell him everything going on at home with the dogs, how his nursery was coming along since I was in the hospital before we could decorate, and even what I had eaten for dinner the night before. Often, our private talks would end up with me in tears and apologizing for my body failing us both and not being able to save his brother. Truthfully, I still keep this guilt with me no matter how many times my husband or therapist tells me that it wasn't my fault. There are just some things that a mother cannot accept, especially in this situation. Especially when it comes to protecting her children.

I would leave around 3:00 pm, knowing our special one-on-one time was over for the day. I would make the drive home to wake up Shawn and tell him what the updates were from the doctors, take the dogs out, eat dinner, pack his lunch for the night, and then we would both drive in separate cars back out to the hospital by 6:00 pm. When Shawn would leave for work by 9:30 pm, I would walk out with him and head home for the night. This routine continued for the next 6 weeks as I lived out my maternity leave with my baby.

There were nights that I would sit in the parking garage after Shawn drove away and realize I was physically holding my breath again. This was my quiet, my reprieve from the day while I was as close as possible to my son in case anything happened. After I could catch my breath, I would go home and climb into bed, exhausted. I was on autopilot and knowing that Colt needed me to be present and be his fighter while he was battling something I couldn't imagine, which was what kept me from falling into the dark hole of losing myself. I can't lie, Shawn and I both started into that hole and while people would ask if we were doing okay or what did we need help with, there wasn't a straightforward answer that wouldn't come off as callous or heartless, so we would both keep our mouths shut and say, "We're okay, but thank you." But the nights that Shawn was home, we would both lay in bed and hold each other while our hearts sank into the mattress. We had fought our hearts out, together, and this is where we were.

There were people at the company I worked for, some whom I had never met before this, who heard about what had happened with our labor, delivery, loss, and struggles and willingly donated their time off to me so that I could spend extra time at home. I cannot express my gratitude to these wonderful people, but I had written each one of them a personal thank you note as it allowed me to stay home an additional 2 weeks before returning to work. I was able to save 4 weeks of my leave so that I could use it when Colt came home, and I could finally be the mom I had expected to be.

Going back to work was significantly difficult, and I expect every parent returning to work after parental leave likely feels this way. Knowing that I couldn't spend my one-on-one time with Colt, and I would miss those daily doctor rotations absolutely gutted me, which I believe was a large contributor to my anxiety that I still battle with. It was at no fault of my workplace; I still needed to provide for my family and no fault of the hospital as they were there to take care of my son. But deep down, I had this overwhelming sense of panic and terror. The additional guilt of not being with Colt, I cannot even begin to describe the feeling a mother has when going to work while their child is in the NICU. But I would leave my house before the sun was up to get to work as early as possible, about 6:00 am, to start my day. I would work non-stop while eating at my desk and only taking breaks to pump, which I was still doing at this point. I would be out the door by 3:00 pm, at the latest, and on the road straight to the hospital. Shawn would meet me there by dinner time, which was usually eaten in the hospital cafeteria or the local spot we had discovered and remain there until 9:30 pm.

Shawn and I have always been very committed and have had a hyper-responsibility mindset to taking care of our kids. When we would walk into that NICU after dinner, the nurses would be bathing the infants and changing their bed linens like clockwork. We never hesitated and learned as soon as we possibly could how to sponge bathe a 3lb infant inside of an incubator with a nasal cannula, heart monitor, and pulse oximeter, while he screamed as he did a backbend the entire time. We knew that Colt was our responsibility, and we couldn't be there throughout the day, so this was our way of taking care of him while the nurses tended to other infants whose parents weren't there daily. Shawn and I worked like a well-oiled machine, taking turns each night on who bathed Colt, changed his diaper, and dressed him while the other changed out the bed sheets and rolls, cleaned the inside walls, and then we would both reapply the fresh stickers and cords he needed for his oxygen or Pulse Ox. We would get to wrap him up in warm blankets and snuggle off and on over the last couple of hours before leaving. One of our favorite books that we would read him almost nightly after his bath is *The Little Engine That Could* by Watty Piper, which I think was more for us than him.

As Colt grew stronger and gained weight, there was a developmental specialist who would come in each week to work with the infants and teach us how to be more proactive in their developmental needs. One of the things that we were encouraged to do was more typical things like bring in a boppy pillow for him to practice tummy time or small toys for him to practice reaching and grabbing. I had even brought in a play gym mat that the nurses would help me set up in his crib once he could successfully maintain his own body temperature and was out of the incubator. Each day, he was growing and thriving, but there were also setbacks during these weeks.

One weekend, I had shown up in the morning, and the doctor had done rounds early that day, so there was a lot of commotion going on. Once things settled down, I pulled Colt out of the incubator to hold him in his tight swaddle and felt something on my chest that seemed off. I had Colt lying on the left side of my chest with his little head tucked under my chin, and I could feel his breathing was irregular. I felt as though I was overreacting, but then I remembered what Debbie said that we are our babies' best advocates and to speak up. I told the nurse something was off, and she said she was grabbing the doctor. The time was going too slow for my expectations, and I kept nudging the nurse to go again and tell the doctor I needed her. Once the doctor came into the pod, she gave me a forlorn look as though I may have been losing it, but to ease my mind, she placed Colt back into the incubator and counted his respirations. I then saw her grab her stethoscope and listen to his tiny body, in which she turned and looked at me and told me that Colt would need to go back off the high-flow nasal cannula (which is where you have the small tubes in your nose pushing air in like you see in the movies), and back onto the NPV. She explained to me that they were going to do a blood draw to accurately check his oxygen levels, which were found to be shockingly low, and he was started on a blood transfusion within the hour. The biggest lesson I learned from these experiences is to unquestionably be your child's champion.

Without a doubt, one of the most terrifying experiences in the NICU is when your child has what they call a "brady." When your baby is less than 36 weeks old, it's not uncommon for an infant to have a brady or bradycardia, and Colt was no exception. The first time Cheyan came to visit in the NICU, Colt was still too critical for anyone else to hold him or even touch him except for Shawn and myself. She couldn't hold her nephew yet but I could so she could see him up close. I sat down in the smaller of the two hospital chairs to hold Colt while she sat in the wooden rocking chair, as she was still pregnant. When the nurse handed me Colt, Cheyan's eyes filled with happy tears, watching me hold my son and knowing we would be doing this together. Then, a brady happened. I knew what they were, as we had been warned not to panic, so I froze. How it was explained to us is that when a preemie falls into a deep sleep, they sometimes forget to breathe. When this happens, it causes a chain reaction of not getting enough oxygen, and their heart rate drops dangerously low. When I heard those alarms start to go off on the monitor above the incubator, the nurse came over quickly and started rubbing Colt's back and feet to pull him out of the deep sleep. I did not take a single breath the entire time I held my baby and watched his heart rate and oxygen drop as far as my stomach had. Cheyan sat there quietly; I was frozen and let the nurse work. Once she got him to respond, I inhaled abruptly; tears poured out of my eyes, and I cried uncontrollably. The nurse and Cheyan rubbed my back and arm to reassure me that Colt was okay, but my heart was not. When I arrived each day, I would ask how many bradys he had that day, and they would give me the number. Often, he had 6 a day, others 2 or 3 times a day. I cried on and off the rest of the evening after I had to tell Shawn what I experienced.

By the time Colt had grown to 4lbs, he was moved off the G-tube. The doctors had now placed an N-tube or a nasal feeding tube that goes from the outside of the nostril and down into the stomach. It became a cute running joke that when we would walk into the pod each day the nurses would tell us how Colt was being mischievous with finding his voice to scream at the nurses for attention or would rip his N-tube out, even though it was taped to his face. Once, Colt wouldn't stop yelling for attention, so the nurses found a Mama-Roo, strapped him in, and let him watch them work for over an hour until he was satisfied. Not much has changed since then; he is still marvelously feisty in every way possible.

Colt would receive most of his nutrition via the N-tube, but he was always moving his mouth like he wanted to eat. So, one day, Debbie was allowed to give him 0.5oz in a dropper to see how he did, as they had to monitor in case he aspirated, but he did remarkably well and would make it known to everyone when he wanted to try to eat by opening his mouth more. Being with Colt in those days, while not as I had planned, was so enjoyable as I got to see my little gummy bear become a child in front of my eyes. He had a fierce personality that I knew would quickly outgrow his little body.

Colt was about 7 weeks old when I walked into the NICU behind someone pushing a strange-looking crib. The crib had white rails that were awkwardly too tall for an infant to get out, very similar to a cage. I stopped at the metal wash tubs and scrubbed my hands all the way up past my elbows, as I did every day and watched this bizarre crib make its way down the hall and into Pod 4. When I went into the pod, the crib was next to Colt's incubator and there was a nurse we hadn't had as one of Colt's caretakers before, but we had seen her around the other pods. She called me over and told me now that Colt had reached 5lbs, they were going to give him a trial run of maintaining his body temperature in an open crib. If he wasn't ready, his body would let us know, and they would simply move him back to the incubator for a couple of days, and we would try again. And that kid did it. Once they moved him to the open crib, he maintained his body temperature and there was no going back.

As the weeks went by, there was no definitive answer of when Colt could come home because he was still too dependent on the machines keeping him alive. There were three rules of thumb that Colt had to learn or develop before coming home. The first was to maintain body temperature, check; he had been doing that for a couple of weeks now. The second was to eat on his own, check; he was eating like a champ; and it was difficult to keep up with his appetite. The third was to breathe on his own, which is where he couldn't manage just yet. The next few weeks became quite the 'norm' for us...go to work, go to the hospital and care for Colt, go to bed, rinse, wash, and repeat.

To break up the monotony, we thought about ways to improve our home situation for when Colt would come home, and the first thought to both of our minds was our bathroom. Our house was small. The main floor had a small living area, a tiny kitchen, and a bathroom so small that you couldn't turn in a full circle without falling over the toilet. The house was old and the pink tile that lined the bathroom had cracked and pushed inward in the shower, and we both knew there was mold back there. Truthfully, if we hadn't touched the wall, it would have likely been fine, but we both feared Colt's precious little lungs would breathe in mold spores and so we decided to tear it all out. Since there hadn't been any talk of when our little boy would come home, we decided to gut the entire bathroom and work on it slowly over the next couple of weeks while we used the bathroom in the basement. The bathroom in the basement was not really a bathroom; in Pittsburgh, it is referred to as a "Pittsburgh bathroom," but it's really an open space with a toilet in the middle of the floor and a dingy shower stall with all the plumbing exposed. It took us two days, from Sunday to Monday, but since Shawn was off work, we gutted that tiny bathroom down to the studs. We started demolition on Sunday, August 28th, and finished cleaning out the debris on Monday, August 29th.

Cue three days later, Thursday, August 31st, 2017. I was sitting in my cube at my desk working on a file when my phone started to vibrate next to my computer mouse. When I looked down and saw "West Penn NICU," my heart sank, and the next breath I remember exhaling was when I stepped into a secluded, unoccupied office, slid the door quietly shut. I fell into a chair, and said, "Hello?" Right then, I heard Sue's voice on the other end; she was one of the physician assistants (PA) at the NICU. She was the most memorable PA we had, that had such an impact on our lives. She had such a connection with Colt and watched him grow, that she became a part of our family while we were there. I knew when I heard her voice that everything was okay, and I could relax. Sue excitedly said, "What do you think about Colt coming home?" I was completely astounded, as we had been told so many times that he was far off from coming home. I repeated myself a couple of times, saying, "What, what do you mean?" And then I heard her warmly laugh and say that one of the doctors said that since Shawn and I have been so hands-on with his care, if we were comfortable with it, he could come home on Tuesday. I grabbed a pen and a yellow post it pad and began writing every little detail that Sue said next. Colt would go to a step-down unit on Monday night where we could stay with him, he would come home with a nasal cannula, oxygen concentrator, pulse oximeter, a band around his chest to count respirations, his medications which included Lasix for the fluid in his lungs, the high caloric formula he needed to help him gain body weight, and the specifics of a car seat test he would have to complete in which he had to keep his oxygen levels up for about an hour while sitting in a car seat. After we hung up, I realized half of my words were scribbled as my hands were shaking. I needed to call Shawn now to tell him what was going on. He was asleep when the phone rang, and when I told him Colt was coming home in a few days, we started making a list of what we needed to do. Then I exclaimed out loud, "Shit, we don't have a bathroom!" and we both started laughing.

Chapter 10

When I left work that day and got to the NICU, Sue was waiting for me so that she and the doctor on shift that day could talk to me about all the things we would need to get moving prior to Colt coming home. My head was swirling.... We had been told almost every day that he was far away from coming home, yet here he was, and I was packing his metaphorical bags to get out of there. The time between that first phone call and getting to the hospital on Monday afternoon is a complete blur. My brain was on autopilot, and we were in lockstep with the hospital on what we needed to do to ensure Colt was coming home safely. When we walked into the hospital that Monday afternoon carrying his car seat, we proudly held our heads high; our son was coming home.

That night in the step-down unit was our first night as full-time parents, and it was rough. Although Colt was a couple of months old at this point, he was used to being up and down throughout the night, constantly hungry, and very vocal. The nurse came in when we first got there to make sure we had enough formula and disposable nipples for the ready-feed bottles, diapers, wipes, and blankets. She let us know that this was our first trial run of managing all his medications and equipment, along with taking on being full-time parents. She said that they would not come into the room unless we called for them or needed help. We understood the assignment. We got through the night, and made sure we could handle everything we were getting thrown into. Except for the lack of sleep that evening, we were able to handle it all. Shawn and I have always been a formidable team when it comes to our little family. The only time the nurse did come in was to do Colt's car seat test, which he failed.

A car seat test is when a baby is hooked up to a pulse ox and strapped into their car seat for 1 hour, in which they must be able to maintain their oxygen levels to safely get from point A to point B. She assured us they would try again in a few hours, but if he failed one more time, he would have to stay there for a couple of days until he could pass. Thankfully, he passed the second time. We were well on our way out of the door when Dr. Elle entered and asked us to sit. His presence was daunting and reassuring all at the same time. He was very forthcoming in telling us that the previous doctor on shift made the decision that Colt could go home, but he was not on board with it. His concern was that Colt still needed a lot of hands-on medical care, and it was a lot to put on his parents when he should be cared for in the hospital. We urged him to let us walk out of those doors with him, knowing we were ready as that was Colt's 99th day of life, and we now had 99 days of experience and reassurance. We had 99 days in the NICU and all 3 of us were ready to just go home. When Dr. Elle was satisfied, he signed the paperwork. We loaded the car seat onto the stroller with the cannula and cords securely wrapped around the handle and all the equipment in the basket underneath. Sept 4th, 2017 was when we walked out of those doors with our son.

We climbed into Shawn's truck and headed home. I sat in the back seat with Colt, keeping my eyes on his oxygen levels, while Shawn drove slowly the entire way. When we walked in the door, both of our dogs were excited to see us as usual. However, they were confused as they could smell the tiny human whose scent was oddly familiar. We had learned the best way to get any pet ready for a new family addition was to bring home things with their scent on them and to lay them around the house. You need the scent to become commonplace so there's nothing drastic or could cause a dog to act out. Shawn was very proactive at this over the prior 3 months...he had brought home blankets and towels each night after washing and holding Colt.

In our small 10'x18' living room, we had a pack 'n' play with a bassinet attached to it against the far wall, which became our saving grace in those early days. Colt would lay in the bassinet and sleep while the equipment was safely off the floor from the dogs and tucked inside, but we became quite the experts in navigating all of the tubes and cords.

As I had mentioned before, one of our biggest adjustments was the cords. There were cords everywhere. Electrical cords from the machines into different outlets, cords from the equipment to Colt's feet and chest, and a nasal cannula taped to his temples. Once we learned how to keep the cords contained so we and the dogs wouldn't trip on them, it was just a part of our daily lives. They became like second limbs to us as we would maneuver around them in moving Colt from room to room and learned some key tips for this type of lifestyle.

Tips for newborns on medical equipment:

1. If you have animals, make sure the equipment can be tucked away and cords up high enough that they won't have the opportunity to pull on them.

2. Always use onesies with snaps; do not buy clothes that require zippers. If you do, their Pulse Ox cord will go all the way up their leg and out of the top near their face, which isn't safe or comfortable.

3. Always make sure to have an extra portable tank of oxygen nearby because moving a large oxygen concentrator throughout the house, like when giving the baby a bath, is not sustainable.

4. Once the baby is strong enough to grab the cannula and pull it from their face over and over, mittens will be your best friend.

Chapter 11

I started my next 4 weeks of leave the day Colt came home. It was the most magical time I could have ever experienced. Colt was up anywhere from two to four times a night, which was a hard learning experience since I technically had a 3-month-old, but I had been sleeping through the night until this point. I developed a new routine and created a schedule so that we could stay on track.

Our daily routine:

1. 6:00 – 6:30 am: Colt would wake up for a bottle.

2. 7:30 – 9:30 am: We would snuggle and play until he would eat again.

3. 10:30 – 12:30 pm: Colt would do tummy time, his play gym, and we would do his stretches until his lunch bottle.

4. 1:00 – 3:00 pm: Colt would nap and then wake up to play. He would nap until about 3:00 pm when he would get up to play some more.

5. 4:00 pm: Colt would have his dinner bottle.

6. 6:00 – 7:30 pm: Colt would get his warm bath, have his last bottle, and go to bed.

With Colt's fragile immune system and underdeveloped lungs, the NICU doctors advised that he could not go to daycare until he was at least 2 years old, which we were fine with because we then became very protective of anyone managing his medications or machines. It was a hard balance, but we made it work somehow. Shawn worked night turn and would stay up with Colt during the day and sleep when Colt slept. I would come home, and Shawn would sleep a few more hours before going to work, and then I would be on evening duty and up throughout the night. It was utterly exhausting, but our son was thriving.

Every couple of weeks, we would load him up into his car seat with all the wires and cords for a trip to either his pediatrician for a routine preemie checkup or to his developmental appointments at West Penn Hospital. These developmental appointments were one of the best things coming out of that experience, as we learned so much and never felt like we were completely on our own. Pediatricians are, of course, helpful in treating your children, but they are nowhere near the experience of the NICU doctors who come down to make the rounds into the developmental clinic to check on your little one's status. And the developmental specialist, who would see us each time, would coach us on the best types of physical exercises or occupational therapy and show us how to do it hands-on. She would weigh and measure Colt during each appointment to make sure he was growing. She would then go through a checklist of milestones that he 'should' be at for his actual age vs. his gestational age. These milestones ranged from lifting his head, turning to look at faces, gripping toys, motor skills, sitting on their own, how they play, and how well they were interacting with the world.

A premature infant has two different ages that physicians use to measure growth. The first is their "actual" age, which is from the day they were born; Colt was born on May 29th. And the second is their "gestational" age, the day they should have been born, which would have been August 10th. So, for instance, when we took Colt into the developmental clinic in October, the specialist would measure how he was doing in comparison as a 4-5-month-old versus his gestational age of 2-3 months old. She would then teach us the skills we needed to help him get to his actual age. We were told that premature kids usually catch up to others of their actual age by the time they turn 2 years old.

We made sure both of us went to each and every appointment, not only because of the luggage we were physically hauling back and forth for each trip but because we never knew what someone would tell us. In one of our late October appointments to the developmental clinic, we were told to start taking Colt's oxygen cannula off for small increments of time, make his lungs work, and monitor his oxygen. This terrified us, of course. But we listened, and slowly, his lungs got stronger since we were making them work on their own and not allowing them to get complacent by relying on oxygen. We went from 10 minutes a day to 20 minutes a day, to eventually an hour.

Colt was scheduled for a surgery on November 1st to repair 3 hernias from his prematurity, which is apparently also quite common in these little ones. When babies are premature, their stomach muscles aren't strong enough to hold their intestines inside of their stomach cavity. So, when they push for a bowel movement or start kicking to move or stretch, the hernias happen. But, because he would be under anesthesia and his body in physical distress, the development specialist and NICU physician told us that we were going to continue the oxygen while practicing breathing room air until after he recovered from the surgery.

While we were at the children's hospital for the surgery, I had a very difficult time allowing the nurses to take him back to the operating room. I was more emotional than I had expected, handing him over and struggling with not being able to physically see him. My sympathetic nervous system kicked in and I started into a full-blown panic attack. Shawn took me down to the cafeteria to get some coffee and tried his best to distract me, but I made him eat quickly so that we could get back up to the waiting room.

Shortly after, the doctor came out to tell us everything went great! Colt had no issues, but they were going to keep him overnight just for observation, and we would be taken to a room shortly. We ended up in a shared room with another child and his parents, so we were more than happy to be discharged the next morning. Thankfully, Colt has no recovery issues, and we were able to move on from this piece of our story.

Chapter 12

Over the next few months, we were blessed to experience our first Thanksgiving, Christmas, and New Year with our little man. He was growing, he was thriving, but he was still behind in his development for his 'actual age.' The specialist at the developmental clinic recommended that we reach out to a program in Pennsylvania called 'Early Intervention' so that we could get some additional help at home.

Early Intervention is an extraordinary program, and I am so grateful for all of their support. The process started out when we had a case worker and occupational therapist assigned to us, who came to our home to meet with us and go over Colt's medical history and assess him, which took a couple of hours for the first meeting. After that, our case worker would assign us specific therapists for Colt's needs.

We started with physical therapy twice a week for one hour. Colt's physical therapist, who we will call Kate, was one of the best humans I have ever met and was so hands-on and kind. She would not only work with him but would talk to us through the sessions and have us practice with Colt so she could watch and coach. When she first arrived, Colt's muscles were so tight that he couldn't reach his own toes. It was explained to us that babies are meant to be curled up into a ball inside the womb until 38-40 weeks of gestation, and when they're premature, their muscles are stretched wide open, so their muscles don't have the elasticity they are supposed to.

Physical therapy lasted for well over a year, in which Kate helped us help Colt to not only touch his toes but to balance to get his knees under him and strengthen his core muscles to sit and even stand. Kate also helped us in getting Colt a helmet for his flat spot that developed from laying in the incubator, and braces for his ankles and feet to allow his muscles to develop correctly so he could walk straight. We were fortunate that Kate would come every week and once Colt was climbing the furniture and jumping across the room, he was able to graduate physical therapy.

Once Colt turned 1-year-old, he began also receiving occupational therapy. His tongue was always slightly sticking out of his mouth, as his tongue muscles weren't strong enough to be able to hold it inside or to bring food into his mouth. We were given special spoons and teething toys for Colt to practice textures and swiping his tongue left to right to strengthen his tongue muscles to be able to bring food to the back of his mouth, instead of it falling out. Shawn and I had learned to feed him his baby food by placing small amounts inside of his cheeks so he would need to swipe to move it appropriately.

Next, we also started nutrition therapy. Since a child's lungs aren't fully developed until they're 8 years old, they use a lot of calories to grow. However, since Colt's lungs were underdeveloped, they not only had to work harder to grow, but to maintain normal breathing, so they would burn large amounts of calories. This was an issue when it came to getting Colt to put on weight, since he could only eat so much at a time, but his lungs would burn it all up. Our nutritional therapist had us start adding Duocal® to Colt's meals, whether his yogurt, milk, or cereal. Duocal® is a very high-calorie supplement that is flavorless but small amounts can help in gaining weight. We also moved him to one PediaSure® a day. However, due to his chronic cough, he would tend to vomit this up during a coughing fit. And let me tell you…regurgitated PediaSure® is the worst smell imaginable to have saturated in your carpet and furniture. Thankfully, we were able to successfully move to whole-fat chocolate milk once a day, as it also has the calories and fat that he needed.

When Colt was about 1.5-2 years old, we began speech therapy. He was thriving in other areas but would still make sounds rather than trying to form words. Our speech therapist would show us which sounds to work on and when, how to encourage him to mimic the sounds, and how to get him to form words. Once he started daycare, his speech therapist even went to daycare once a week to work with him on-site.

The amount of appreciation we have for the Early Intervention program is limitless, as they helped us get Colt to where he needed to be as a normal little boy. When you meet Colt, you would never know he was premature as he is taller than most kids, one of the top readers in his class, and never stops talking.

Chapter 13

When Colt was about 10 months old, I was in the kitchen and was pouring myself a glass of milk. Shawn walked in and looked at me sideways, knowing I hated drinking milk, except when I was pregnant. He looked at me jokingly and said, "Are you pregnant?"

My first response was, "What? No way!"

Shawn and I were back to being a regular married couple and being intimate, but I was also on birth control, so I didn't think twice about the milk. However, a couple days later, I caught myself drinking more milk. I decided that while Shawn was at the store and Colt was napping, I would use one of the pregnancy tests just to double check, since I was not in a good space mentally for another baby. We were still learning to balance our new lives of rotating work schedules while caring for Colt, trying to work through our grief of losing Lucas when we had a moment, and being confined to the house since we couldn't go to public places with a sick infant.

After I laid Colt down, I walked into the bathroom and peed on the stick. It was an instant 'Pregnant' on the test, and I began shaking. I had an immediate panic attack with the increased heart rate, sweating, diarrhea, and ultimate feeling of pending doom. Thankfully, Shawn had pulled up and was standing outside in his truck when I finally came out of the bathroom holding the test in my hand. He saw my sobbing through the door and came running up to hug me, and then busted out laughing when he saw the positive test.

Once I started to calm down, it hit me like a brick wall, and I would get worked up all over again. I called my OB/GYN and asked them to please do an ultrasound as soon as possible, as I didn't know how far along I was, and I NEEDED to know how many babies were inside of me. But they wouldn't see me for at least another 4-5 weeks when I was estimated to be between 8 to 9 weeks pregnant. That wait was excruciatingly slow, but the appointment went better than expected.

The doctor was able to confirm that I was 9 weeks pregnant with a single baby! That was the first moment I felt myself become excited, and when I left the office, I felt like I was on cloud 9. A pregnancy that I could do my best to enjoy. However, after the next few weeks, I'm not sure if it was the extra rush of hormones, the fear of having to go through the same sequences of events as before, or the lack of sleep I was experiencing, but I knew my mental state was not where it should be.

Shawn and I were still trying to balance our grief with our joy; however, I kept thinking about my sweet first baby that we lost, Lucas. I was fixated on how he had to be so lonely, and it was so unfair to him that we were trying to be happy and now we were bringing another baby into the mix. My heart was so heavy that I reached out to a therapist. During my first appointment, when I spilled my guts, she told me all my feelings were 'normal' and 'justified.' She said that I would continue to 'just heal.' I left that appointment feeling insulted. As a pregnant woman who suffered so much pain, I was practically yelling for help, and no one was helping. I would cry while rocking Colt to sleep, holding this perfect little boy. Then I would cry every time Shawn had to leave, I would cry every time I had to wake up and get out of bed, and I would cry during my hour-long drive home from work. I needed help, and I knew that I was spiraling. One night when Shawn was home, I broke down and told him that it's not fair that Lucas has to be alone while Colt and our new baby will have both parents. I also told him that I felt like I needed to be with Lucas, he needed his mom and then all our children would have a parent to love them and hold them.

Shawn encouraged me to try again, but this time to call Allegheny Women's Behavioral Health. I wasn't okay for myself or for my family. During my first appointment with my new doctor, I explained to her that I didn't want to be alive anymore. I wanted to be with Lucas, but I couldn't allow myself to leave Colt either. She agreed that I needed help and that it would get harder before it got easier, but after some time, I was diagnosed with postpartum disorder, post-traumatic stress disorder (PTSD), and anxiety.

Thankfully, we were able to start some pregnancy-safe medications in addition to the therapy sessions. It took several months to get the dosage correct, but as time passed, I started to feel slightly normal again. Colt was almost sleeping through the night when we found out I was having another boy. My hormones started to balance out, and I was learning grief techniques through my therapist. I needed to come to a full acceptance that I had lost my baby and that it truly wasn't my fault that he died, and to continuously talk about him and keep his memory on top of my mind because I love him just as I love his little brothers.

Chapter 14

My second pregnancy was going well, except for being diagnosed with gestational diabetes. When friends or family would find out, I would get the obligatory 'I'm sorry to hear that,' but it was no big deal to me. I had dealt with much worse and even had gestational pregnancy before. If this was all I was to have, piece of cake.

But, because of the gestational diabetes, my baby was on the bigger side and my doctor scheduled my c-section for December 18th. We walked in, and I'm fairly certain that I was going into natural labor as I felt some contractions that morning. Shawn tried to get the doctors to let me try naturally, but since it was already scheduled, they didn't want to take the chance of needing the surgery later and chose to move ahead with my c-section that morning.

Rhett Timothy Salopek was born at 9:21 am on December 18th, 2018. He was 8lb 8oz and the most rosy, red cherub I have ever seen; he was perfection. I held onto my little boy skin-to-skin for the next 4 hours and wouldn't let anyone take him. Eventually, I had to let Shawn do some skin-to-skin time with him before our families came to visit and meet our littlest man. One of my favorite memories is when Colt walked in to see Rhett and didn't know what was going on... He smiled so big, then stuck his finger right into Rhett's mouth. I had two of my little boys in my arms, and I had never felt more peaceful.

Shawn was able to stay the first night in the hospital with me but needed to go home the second night to take care of Colt. That second night was rough, to say the very least. Rhett was a very affectionate baby and needed to be constantly held or else he'd scream like a banshee. However, the nurses wouldn't let you sleep if you were holding your baby, but my baby would scream every time I put him down. I literally had to stay awake throughout the night to hold him, or I'd be woken up to him screaming anyways. I was so exhausted, and when I asked to send him to the nursery, the nurse on staff told me no! She told me they don't like to do that and my baby needed to stay with me. After a few more sleepless hours, so much pain from the c-section and a few hundred tears later, the nurse agreed to take Rhett to the nursery until his next feeding. This means I had about 2 hours to get some sleep.

The next day, when Shawn came to get us, I was utterly exhausted. Shawn and I made an agreement that he would get up with Colt throughout the night, and I would sleep in the living room with Rhett's bassinet next to me, as the couch was easier to get up from with the c-section still healing. Those first few nights, I can count on one hand how much sleep I got and all the tears...being a mom with a newborn is so so hard. I would gladly have more children if I could skip the stressful pregnancy stage and the first 3-4 months of the newborn stage. Hand me a child around 4 months old, and we're golden.

Shawn returned to work a couple of weeks later, and I got the full experience of what it would have been like to have two little ones from the very beginning. Chaotic, but so very perfect. Shawn was often mandated into working 16-hour days, so there were weeks we'd barely see each other. I'd have the boys from sunup to sunup...you read that correctly. Sunup to sunup because they never seem to sleep at the same time. There were times I would think they planned it on purpose, just to torture me...but it was so worth it. The giggles and snuggles I would get from both; my heart was so happy.

After Rhett was 3 months old and Colt was just under 2 years old, we decided to try them both in daycare. We got the 'all clear' from the developmental clinic to send Colt, as he was more than thriving and needed to start letting his immune system develop. Shawn and I were both sick with anxiety, leaving our little boys at daycare. So, for the first day, we both took off work to give it a trial run. Not surprisingly, they both did amazing! So, our next journey started. Shawn went to work, I returned to work full-time, and the kids started daycare. We were almost like an ordinary family, with a few exceptions mixed in.

Chapter 15

It's true that my life has not been easy, as I don't think anyone has an easy life. However, I do believe that the way you respond to a situation makes all the difference in how you enjoy your life. Understanding our limits is not a failure. In fact, it is a sign of pure strength because only then can you know what you can and cannot do, and what you need in order to move on. Yes, I am still very stubborn and I still like to be as independent as I can. But, I also know when to slow down and ask for help or other people's opinions in unfamiliar territory. I know that appreciating other people's experiences and opinions is what makes the world go round, and we simply cannot have a fulfilling life without one another.

I've had women ask me about my journey, and I can now talk openly and calmly about it, wanting them to know that they aren't alone. I enjoy talking about my 3 children, the things I've learned along the way, and what I can share with others. Whether you've experienced joy, loss, grief, happiness, loneliness, or uncertainty of your feelings, I can guarantee that whether the situation causing those feelings is different than others, the feelings are similar. You are not alone; we are in this together.

Chapter 16

I would like to share some of my personal stories below between myself and my children that I have written down along the way. I want to show that how you respond to terrible circumstances can help your soul to heal and your heart to allow so much joy and laughter in...

November 14th, 2019

899 Days. It has been 899 days since Colt and Lucas were born. 899 days of heartbreak, love, hope, teamwork, of the unknown. When Colt was born, he fought to live. He made it through ALL of that. He was in the NICU for 99 days, came off oxygen by 6 months, and didn't lose any vision from being on oxygen. He has his hearing and only had a sub-1 brain bleed that subsided, then he had therapy. He went to the BPD Clinic and then to the developmental

clinic. He's had physical therapy, he had occupational therapy for eating, developmental therapy, and speech therapy. Well, today he had this therapy review, and he NO LONGER QUALIFIES! He graduated from the last of it today, hitting above average on all of his marks.

This child is a miracle. He loves to run and jump. He talks up a storm in asking questions and telling stories (he's talking at a 3-year-old level); he understands way more than he should. 899 days of fighting and now he's done and can be a normal, healthy, happy kid. Day 900 is a whole new world for our little family.

August 23rd, 2020

There is quite literally no fear like it...

Picture it...

Setting: 1:42 am, everyone is asleep, and the house is pitch dark.

You're dead asleep and hear a toy in the living room making a noise like the batteries are dying. You get up out of bed and go to find the toy in the dark living room (I didn't put my glasses on) so that it doesn't wake up your husband, who has to be up for work soon. You go into the living room and all the noise suddenly stops. Silence. You walk over to the kid's toy food truck, bend down to listen for it, and hear a tiny whisper in the pitch dark. "Hi, Mommy." I nearly jumped out of my skin!!

What did I find; a 3-year-old little boy who snuck out of the room, down the stairs, climbed the child gate, and is now playing in the food truck, butt naked! I then had to get him back in his room, find him some clothes (I couldn't find his first set of pjs) and explain to him why he can't sneak downstairs in the middle of the night. I'm still catching my racing heart!

Edit: 6:52 am – I just found a half-eaten tomato on the living room carpet and his pants by the kitchen sink!

October 9th, 2017

We don't normally hold Colt and rock him to sleep at night; we snuggle him until he gets sleepy, feed him, change him, and then put him in his crib, where he looks around or stretches until he falls asleep. Well, yesterday, I was going through his clothes and putting the ones he's outgrown into storage, and I cried the entire time.

It was so bittersweet holding up these tiny little preemie clothes that I'd put off putting into storage. These clothes are so small you can't believe your child was too small for at one point, when he was too small to eat on his own, to breathe on his own, the clothes he wore when we were maybe allowed to split an hour of time a day to hold him as long as he was having a good day and could tolerate the feel of our arms, the sound of our voices, being against our chest, or listening to our hearts beat.

Then, there were his newborn clothes, these clothes that he's been in for months that he's not getting too round for, too long for. The tears just flowed as I walked into the living room to show Shawn these itty bitty clothes as he held our 10lb son asleep on his chest. Happy tears filled my eyes because Colt has come so far. Our little 4.5-month-old who is finally moving into 0-3 clothes, who can hold his head up, our itty bitty little babu who is learning to roll over and loves to smile and 'talk' to Mommy and Daddy. Yet, also sad tears because he's getting bigger and one day won't be my tiny little boy who smiles when I kiss him goodnight and put him in his crib. So tonight, after I fed him each time and changed his diaper, I held him a little longer, I sang a little longer, I rocked him until his eyes drifted off to sleep, and then gave him 100 extra kisses as I'm so grateful he's growing, thriving, and ours.

February 4th, 2021

Funny things my kids have said lately:

First, we were having a dance party earlier today...

Me: Alexa, play 'Baby' by Justin Bieber.

Rhett: Dustin Butter Weiner?

At bedtime, I was getting the kids dressed..

Colt: Mommy, I love boobies.

Me: What?! Whose boobies?!

Colt: All the boobies.

Me: where...what...who?!

February 10th, 2021

I was putting Colt to bed tonight, and he said the sweetest thing.

Me: Colt, I love you so much, baby.

Colt: Mommy, I'm not a baby.

Me: No matter how big you get, you are my baby.

Colt: No, Mommy, I'm not a baby…but I love you so much, too; you give pretty good hugs.

March 6th, 2021

Rhett was standing on the big chair in Colt's room.

Me: Rhett, get down so you don't get hurt.

Rhett: *No!*

Colt: Rhett, get down or you gotta go to the doctor.

Me: That's right, get down, Rhett!

Colt: Rhett, you will have to go to the doctor and they will say you don't listen so they will pull your big toe off, they'll rip it off with scissors and then take your eyes and throw them away!

Well, that escalated quickly…but Rhett got down.

May 10th, 2021

Shawn and I are still laughing at this. The boys were getting ready for bed, and Rhett went to get his binkie.

Shawn: Rhett, you don't need that. Come here, I need a hug!

Rhett: (dead-faced, turns to Shawn) That's your problem.

February 17th, 2022

Each night, we've been doing games with the kids to keep them active or thinking—hide and seek, tag, basketball, superhero fights, and counting on the swings. The other night, I asked Colt if I could teach him how to play duck, duck, goose.

Me: Colt, can I teach you to play duck, duck, goose tomorrow? I don't think you've ever played it.

Colt: (gives me the side eye) That sounds like you eat a duck and fart out a quack.

September 20th, 2022

As I got the kids in a bath tonight, I did my best to absorb the little details. I usually notice the height difference from the night before. The baby features, slowly but surely, fading with each passing night. Tonight, I felt a pain, a sadness in my chest about how strongly I miss Colt. This big kid was standing in front of me and making me hysterically laugh, and yet I was missing him. Then, I realized why I dreaded Kindergarten so much; I knew he would grow faster.

The days go faster. The weeks speed by, and the weekends just fade. His poor little mind is not just worried about which snacks to eat, what trap to build with his bungee cords, and how tall he can build his blocks, but now, he's thinking about reading, counting, and writing. He doesn't have toddler problems anymore, and my heart misses his heart. That innocence and always needing mommy, that heart. After tucking them in, I went and laid with him. We talked about his book fair at school and laughed about something he had to tell me about SpongeBob and his plans to ride a buggy the next day. And then I lay there. I lay there until he was sound asleep; I continued to lay there. I am not ready for him to be 1 more day older. My sweet little Colty.

October 19th, 2022

I swear kids like to hear you yell. Tonight, the boys were in the bath, and Colt went to dump out the soap.

Me: (calmly) Colt, don't. Colt, stop. (Now yelling) Stop! Colt Michael!

Colt: Why did you yell?

Me: Why do I have to repeat myself 10 times before I have to yell at you?

Colt: Because you know who I am.

December 27th, 2022

The Salopek boys saga continues...

A few months ago, I told Colt to stop being so difficult. (I don't remember what the task was that we were trying to complete.)

Rhett looks me dead in the face and says: If he is diffi-Colt, then I am diffi-Rhett.

I haven't thought much of it until tonight.

Rhett wouldn't stop throwing things, so I said: *Rhett, why don't you listen?*

His response: Oh, you know, I'm diffi-Rhett.

* * *

To my boys – Thank you for making me a mama, I will fight for you until my last breath. No matter what we've been through, you are the light of my world and fill my heart with so much love.

About the Author

Sarah Salopek considers herself a 'regular mom' and is often seen at the bus stop in her sweatpants and a hot cup of coffee in hand. She is a mother, wife, daughter, sister, and friend who loves to connect with her loved ones. She enjoys doing crafts, cooking family dinners, reading thriller mysteries, and challenging herself to learn new skills. Sarah grew up in Pittsburgh where she now lives with her family of four and their two dogs.